Salvation Is from the Catholic Church

How Christ Uses the Church to Bring Us to Him

Trent Horn

© 2025 Trent Horn

All rights reserved. Except for quotations, no part of this book may be reproduced or transmitted in any form or by any means, electronic or mechanical, including photocopying, recording, uploading to the internet, or by any information storage and retrieval system without written permission from the publisher.

Unless otherwise noted, Scripture quotations are from the Revised Standard Version of the Bible, copyright © 1946, 1952, and 1971 National Council of the Churches of Christ in the United States of America. Used by permission. All italics in Scripture quotes are the author's.

All rights reserved worldwide.

Published by Catholic Answers, Inc.
2020 Gillespie Way
El Cajon, California 92020
1-888-291-8000 orders
619-387-0042 fax
catholic.com

Printed in the United States of America

Cover design by eBookLaunch.com
Interior design by Nora Malone

978-1-68357-403-3
978-1-68357-404-0 Kindle
978-1-68357-405-7 ePub

Contents

Introduction

The apostle Paul said in 1 Corinthians 13:11, "When I was a child, I spoke like a child, I thought like a child, I reasoned like a child; when I became a man, I gave up childish ways."

Well, when I was a child, I thought you got to heaven by just being a nice person.

My parents never took me to church, and the closest "Sunday school education" I received was from old Bible cartoons produced by the same animation company that made *The Flintstones*. I thought they were fun stories, but by high school, that's all I thought they were: stories.

In my teen years, I believed in God but thought religion was for simpletons. I thought it was time to "put away childish things." Fortunately, that all changed after some of my Christian friends urged me to consider the evidence for their faith.

I devoured the religion section of our school library and downloaded as many debates between Christians and atheists as I could on my parents' slow dial-up internet. About six months into my journey, my idea of God went from an unknown "first cause" to a Trinity of persons, one of whom became incarnate as the man Jesus Christ. I started calling myself a Christian, but I faced a dilemma: although my Catholic friends had brought me to faith in Christ, to me it seemed that their religion complicated Jesus' simple gospel with unnecessary rules and rituals.

Even after they invited me to attend Mass, I kept thinking, *Why would I need to go to Mass, or say the rosary, or worry about purgatory, or go to confession? Isn't the Bible clear on this? Believe in Jesus, and you will be saved.*

As I studied the Bible, however, I saw that it didn't present a clear answer to the question "How do I get to heaven?" Every time I found one passage that seemed to offer a simple answer, I would find another, sometimes in the same book or letter in the New Testament, that gave a different answer. Eventually, I saw that the Christian system of salvation didn't make sense apart from the *Church*: the one, holy, catholic, and apostolic Church that Jesus founded.

Saved by *Catholicism*?

I can imagine a lot of people saying to me, "Salvation doesn't come the Catholic Church. It doesn't come from *any* church! Salvation comes from the blood of Jesus Christ!"

I see where they're coming from.

It wasn't the Catholic Church that was crucified for my or your sins. It wasn't the Catholic Church that rose from the dead to justify me before God. It was Jesus Christ who did those things. That's why the *Catechism of the Catholic Church* (CCC) says that "all salvation comes from Christ the head through the Church which is his body" (846).

The Bible says that the church of the living God is the *pillar and foundation of truth* (1 Tim. 3:15). Many of us first heard the gospel from a leader or member of a church—like a pastor, a missionary, or our own parents. As St. Paul writes, "How are they to believe in him of whom they have never heard? And how are they to hear without a preacher?" (Rom. 10:14). And to be obedient to Christ, Christians usually seek out someone in a church (usually a pastor) to baptize them instead of just baptizing themselves. Most also feel that it is their duty to attend a "good" and "Christian" church.

But which one?

In this book, I will show that salvation in Jesus Christ requires obedience to Christ *and* to the one visible Church Christ established for the purpose of gathering the entire human race into God's new covenant. That's because Catholic doctrine contains the complete answer to the question, "What must I *do* to be saved?"

Having said that, let me share a bit more about what this book is *not*.

It is not a systematic or comprehensive explanation of the doctrine of salvation, or what theologians call *soteriology*. I'll explain, as much as I can in a single volume, why Catholic teaching on salvation is true, but I won't be answering every objection to Catholicism (I've addressed the major ones in my book *The Case for Catholicism*). I also won't be getting into the finer details of things like predestination or justification. Instead, the emphasis will be on what we must *do* to be saved and how the Catholic Church is the instrument through which God saves us.

I also won't spend time defending the basics of Christian belief—for example, that Jesus is the God-Man who died for our sins and rose from the dead. I've defended the core elements of the gospel in other works, so we'll start from the premise that the gospel is true and then explore the question "What must I do to be saved?"

The first part of this book will present ten things we must do to be saved that come to us through the Catholic Church, which shows how salvation comes from the Catholic Church. The second part of this book will then answer common objections non-Catholics have toward the Catholic view of salvation.

First, we will address objections based on the idea that there is nothing we must do after our initial salvation, because a true Christian can never lose his salvation. Then, we will deal with objections to the Catholic belief that, in order to be saved, we must remain in union with the one, holy, catholic, and apostolic Church that Christ established.

If you're Catholic, you might be nodding your head in agreement with what you just read. Or maybe you're shaking your head, wanting to understand it all better. And if you are not Catholic, you're probably feeling skeptical. So, to you now I offer the words of the prophet Isaiah: "Come, let us reason together" (Isa. 1:18).

PART I

Ten Ways Salvation Comes Through the Church

CHAPTER 1

Right *Beliefs*

The Catholic Church teaches what we must believe in order to be saved.

After college, I traveled the country with a pro-life organization whose staff were evenly divided between Catholics and Protestants. This made for interesting conversations around the trays of lasagna we ate in the evenings. (If you've ever had to feed thirty missionaries, you understand the utility of lasagna.)

One night, we were having a slightly technical discussion about specific topics related to salvation—such as whether justification involves an "infused" or "imputed" righteousness—when an older man who was friends with our dinner host politely inserted himself into the conversation:

"Look, I don't know about all this theology stuff. I'm just a simple man, and I know that when the jailer asked Paul, 'What must I do to be saved?,' Paul just said to believe in Jesus. I love all you Catholics here, but Paul didn't say anything about the pope, or purgatory, or rosaries. Just believe in Jesus, and you will be saved."

The Simple Catholic Plan of Salvation

This man isn't alone in his attitude toward Catholicism. I remember reading one Protestant website that described the

"Catholic plan of salvation" as containing over *fifty* steps, whereas the "biblical plan of salvation" is just an arrow drawn from "faith in Christ" to "eternal life in heaven." The attitude could be summed up like this: "God loves us, so he made it simple to understand how to get to heaven. The Catholic view of salvation is anything but simple. Therefore, being Catholic must not be God's plan for our salvation."

It's a common attitude, but it's not accurate.

Catholic teaching on salvation *is* biblical, and it *can* be easily summarized. It only *seems* complicated if you try to list every single action a person must do or not do to be saved. Moreover, many Protestant plans of salvation would seem just as complicated if they listed everything people *will do* as a sign that they are saved.

Let's start with the claim that Catholicism overcomplicates salvation.

As support for this claim, Protestants mention things like the sacraments, the papacy, rosaries, purgatory, indulgences, and many other parts of Catholic doctrine or spirituality. Unfortunately, even some well-meaning Catholics contribute to this misunderstanding when they say that Protestants believe in salvation "by faith alone" (Latin: *sola fide*), whereas Catholics believe we are saved by "faith and works." But the Catholic Church does not simplistically teach that we are saved by a combination of "faith and works."

When I explain the Church's plan of salvation, I put it this way: *Repent, Receive, and Remain*. Here's how it has worked in my own life.

The Three Rs of Salvation

During my conversion in high school, I *repented* of my sins and *received* Jesus Christ into my life. Today, I live out my faith in the knowledge that, if I *remain* united to Christ until death, I will enter into heavenly glory with him.

That's all of it: repent, receive, and remain.

You don't have to pray the rosary to be saved. You don't have to perform a certain number of "good deeds" to be saved. And you don't have to receive all seven sacraments to be saved. (Very few Catholics have ever done that, anyway.) Just repent, receive, and remain.

One reason Protestants and Catholics often talk past each other on the issue of salvation is that many Protestants view salvation as a single moment in our lives—the instant they "got saved." Catholics agree that there *is* a single moment in our lives when we go from being a condemned sinner to being a saved child of God. That's why I referred in the past tense to having *repented* and then *received* Jesus Christ when I was in high school.

But Catholics also recognize that salvation is a *process*. It doesn't consist only of the moment we go from being damned to being "saved." It has a "first moment" and a "last moment." Our process of salvation continues throughout our lives, as we choose to remain united to Christ until we die and then go to be with him. That's why Paul speaks of "the gospel, which you received, in which you stand, by which you are saved, *if you hold it fast*—unless you believed in vain" (1 Cor. 15:1-2).

Catholics believe in the gospel. We believe we are saved by the life, death, and resurrection of Jesus Christ, and that this is good news! Catholics and Protestants agree that Jesus' victory over death is good news that we accept through faith; we just disagree on how God wants us to respond to that good news.

One of those big differences is on what you must believe to be saved. Whereas Protestants say Catholics overcomplicate salvation, many Protestants, especially "non-denominational"

Christians, dangerously understate what we must believe to be saved. And this is where we see the first reason salvation comes from the Catholic Church: the Church reveals what we must believe to be saved.

Bill and Ted's Evangelistic Adventure

Remember the older man at our lasagna dinner? "Just believe in Jesus, and you will be saved." Well, let's test that idea.

Suppose a missionary named Bill shares the gospel with an atheist named Ted. Ted sees that his life is not a cosmic accident but was created by a God who loves him. Ted is sorry for his sins and asks what he needs to do to go heaven. Bill tells him, "Just believe in Jesus, and you will be saved."

A week later, Ted comes back saying he joined a wonderful church that preaches Jesus Christ. It's even called The Church of Jesus Christ . . . of Latter-day Saints. Bill frowns, utters a deep sigh, and tells Ted that this "church" is a part of the non-Christian Mormon religion (i.e., Mormonism).

"Mormonism teaches a false Jesus that cannot save. To be saved, you have to believe that there is one God and that Jesus is fully man and fully God, but Mormons believe that men can become gods, Jesus is a mere creature, and the devil is Jesus' brother!"[1]

The next week, Ted sees Bill again and says, "Don't worry, Bill! I found a great church this time. They believe in one God and that Jesus is fully God and fully man. In fact, they baptize people in the name of Jesus because Jesus is the center of everything they do."

"Oh, no," Bill says as he shakes his head. "Ted, it sounds like you joined a group of Oneness Pentecostals."

"Yeah, what's wrong with that?"

"What's wrong is that, like Mormons, they aren't Christian."

"But they believe in one God, Jesus Christ!" Ted fires back.

"Yeah, but they deny the Trinity. They think the Father, Son, and the Holy Spirit are really the same person who manifests in different modes, like how a man can be a father, a son, and an uncle at the same time. They deny that the true God is one being who exists as three distinct, equally divine persons: Father, Son, and Holy Spirit."

Another week goes by, and Ted returns to Bill.

"Okay, Bill, I started going to a Catholic church. They believe in the Trinity and Christ's full divinity. So, am I saved?"

Bill lets out a long sigh. "No, because they reject that we are saved by faith alone. They preach a false gospel."

Ted loses his composure and blurts out, "I thought you said all I had to do to be saved was believe in Jesus! Now you're saying I have to believe in other things like the Trinity or salvation by faith alone. Is there anything else I need to do to be saved that you forgot to tell me?"

Bill and Ted's adventure could span a whole book of conversations. As you'll see, Protestants don't agree on what a person must believe to be saved. This creates problems with believers who struggle with certain Christian doctrines but still want to be saved.

The Bible "Demolition Man"

Craig is a Protestant I know who "deconstructed." The term often refers to someone questioning his faith to the point that he no longer can call himself a Christian.

From my perspective, Craig's loss of faith wasn't a deconstruction; it was a violent *destruction* or *demolition* of the soul. But such a spiritually gory process does sound pretty tame when you call it "deconstruction"—like taking apart your favorite LEGO set.

When I asked Craig what pushed him over the edge, he said it was studying the Bible.

"The more I debated atheists online, the more I realized I didn't have all the answers," he told me. "I was so certain that evolution was false and that the world was created in six days. But after studying biology in college, I saw it was all wrong. The Bible is just what ignorant ancient people thought the world looked like. How could I keep believing it?"

"But the choice isn't young earth creationism or atheism," I replied. "Why not believe that Genesis literally describes who made the world—God—but uses non-literal language to describe how he made the world?"

"But how far will that go?" Craig asked. "I also don't think the Virgin Birth is historical. Can I believe that that is non-literal and still be saved?"

"Well, you can't do *that*."

. . . to which Craig blurted out, "Who says?!"

Who says, indeed.

In the early twentieth century, critical scholarship began to cast doubt on the historicity of the Virgin Birth, and some liberal Protestants said Christians could accept this scholarship and still be saved. Other Protestants denied this and wrote a series of essays called *The Fundamentals: A Testimony to the Truth*. They said a Christian cannot reject the doctrine of Christ's virgin birth. But even those who opposed theological liberalism had to face the problem of defining which beliefs are necessary for salvation and which are not. J. Gresham Machen, one of the foremost defenders of the Virgin Birth in the early twentieth century, said, "Who can tell exactly how much knowledge of the facts about Christ is necessary if a man is to have saving faith? None but God can tell."[2]

Since God can mercifully save anyone, we can't say any particular individual is damned because of his beliefs or actions. Only

God know the person's eternal fate. But Machen's argument is more that denying the Virgin Birth leads to a false, materialist worldview, not that the denial itself is damnable. That's why he says, "Even if the belief in the Virgin Birth is not necessary to every Christian, it is certainly necessary to Christianity. And it is necessary to the corporate witness of the Church."[3]

The difficulty that arises among Protestants is that there is no universal teaching mechanism to arbitrate these theological disputes and determine which beliefs are necessary not just for the Church's witness, but for every believer. That's why the Catholic Church, infallibly teaches that the truth "Christ was born of the Virgin Mary" is a part of God's revelation. Therefore, willfully rejecting this truth constitutes the sin of heresy and puts a person's soul in grave danger.

But what is heresy, and why is it dangerous to our souls?

Hunting Heresy

We normally think of "heresy" as a wrong religious belief, but the original use of the word *hairesis* focused on belonging to a wrong religious group, not a wrong belief.

When the Jewish priests opposed Paul before the Roman governor Felix, they said Paul was "a ringleader of the sect [*hairesis*] of the Nazarenes" (Acts 24:5). In his defense before Felix, Paul said, "I admit to you, that according to the Way, which they call a sect [*hairesis*], I worship the God of our fathers, believing everything laid down by the law or written in the prophets" (Acts 24:14). And in Galatians 5:19-21, Paul lists several works of the flesh (in contrast to fruits of the Spirit), one of which is *hairesis*, which is usually translated "dissensions" or "factions."

Among Catholics, the sin of heresy often follows the sin of rejecting the Church's teaching authority, or the sin of schism (which we will discuss in chapter seven). It's not uncommon for a person to become a heretic after joining a denomination that broke away from the Church, since he ends up following the error that caused the denominational split in the first place. For example, the Protestant Reformers had some legitimate concerns about corrupt or sinful practices within the Church's leadership, which were addressed at the ecumenical Council of Trent a few decades later. But this "reformation" quickly became a "revolution," with those who rejected the Church's authority accusing one another of heresy. Calvinists and Lutherans even recommended that anabaptists, who rejected infant baptism, be executed through the ironic punishment of drowning.[4]

Modern Protestantism, with its untold number of distinct denominations, tends to downplay the sin of "dissension." Under Protestantism, "the church" is a loose confederation of denominations united in a vague set of "core Christian beliefs." A group that rejects one of these core beliefs, like how Mormons reject the Trinity, would be placed outside the realm of Protestantism. However, although Protestants can often cite a handful of essential doctrines like the Trinity or Christ's divinity, they don't agree on what criterion determines which doctrines are so essential to the Christian faith that willfully denying them entails the sin of heresy.

For example, a doctrine can't be heretical merely because a person thinks it contradicts Scripture. Calvinists think non-Calvinist views contradict Scripture, and non-Calvinists think the same about Calvinists. But hardly any Protestant would say a person is an unsaved heretic merely because he got Calvinism wrong. They'd say the same about the age of the earth or the cessation of charismatic gifts. These are secondary issues that do not affect a person's faith if he gets the Bible wrong about them. They are not the "main things," which Protestants say the Bible presents as "plain things" that all Christians are required to believe.

But not all theological topics fall neatly or plainly into "essential" or "non-essential."

It's essential to believe that Christ was truly man, but do you have to believe that Christ had a human mind, or a human will? Denying that Christ has these human faculties leads to heresies that were condemned at the Church's ecumenical councils (universal gatherings of the bishops). These were the same councils that gave us the Nicene Creed, which some denominations refuse to recite in their services.[5]

Do you have to believe in original sin to be a Christian? How about Christ being the Son before the Incarnation? Or that eternal damnation is a real possibility and universalism is false? There are self-proclaimed Protestants who deny each of these doctrines and others who accept them but feel as though they are still acceptable for Christians to debate.

However, when the Catholic Church infallibly *defines* a doctrine, it brings debate about the doctrine to "an end"—or in Latin, *de fine*. Without such an authority, Protestantism becomes a body of knowledge that is "always reforming," and so no doctrine is safe from Christians who feel as though the Church got something wrong—be it the Reformers, who overturned 1,500 years of teaching; Evangelicals, who overturned 1,800 years of doctrine, including ones held by mainline Protestants; or modern liberal Protestants, who consider nothing taught over the past 2,000 years to be inviolate or beyond "reform."

This also complicates the Protestant claim that one must simply "believe the gospel" to be saved, since Protestants have no authority to define what "the gospel" even is. The New Testament references the gospel but doesn't explicitly describe it. The closest it comes to that is in 1 Corinthians

15, where Paul discusses Christ's death for our sins and his resurrection. But believing this isn't enough for salvation, since there is no mention in this chapter of Christ's divinity or the triune nature of God.

And some Protestants expand the meaning of "the gospel" to include false doctrines whose denial, they ironically charge, constitutes the promotion of a false gospel.

For example, many Protestants say "the gospel" includes the claim that the Father literally punished Jesus on the cross in our place by pouring out his wrath upon the Son. This is called the *penal substitution* theory of the atonement, and Catholics, along with many Protestants, reject this view. They would favor other views, like that Christ offered himself as a perfect sacrifice of love that makes up for the debt incurred by our sins and that the Father did not literally punish an innocent person for our sins.

The problem for the Protestant view of salvation is that their only infallible authority is a collection of writings that never give a list, or even a general criterion, of which doctrines are essential for salvation and which are not. This leaves believers to do their best to discern what Scripture teaches on this matter, which leads, as we've seen, to unacceptably divergent viewpoints.

Founding Fathers (of the Faith)

The Catholic Church defines heresy in a similar way to "essential doctrines" but uses the following technical definition: the obstinate post-baptismal denial of some truth which must be believed with divine and catholic faith (CCC 2089). Someone who joins a non-Catholic faction or dissension (*hairesis*) against the Catholic Church often ends up believing a "heresy" as a result because he has spurned the Church's wisdom, which is safeguarded by the Holy Spirit.

Here's an analogy to help understand why God gave us the Church to be the instrument of our salvation when it comes to teaching the faithful what they must believe.

The founding fathers of the United States wanted the Constitution to be the framework for the laws of their new country. But if each citizen decides for himself what the Constitution means, then the country could exist in name only. Instead, they had the foresight to create a Supreme Court that would have the ultimate authority to settle disputes about the Constitution, including how to apply it to situations in the far future beyond what the founding fathers would have envisioned.

God has done something similar with the Bible. Instead of giving his church a fallible Supreme Court, he gave it an infallible Magisterium, a living teaching office. The teachings of the Council of Jerusalem were binding the moment the apostles uttered them, and not only when they finally were recorded in Scripture (Acts 15). As we'll see in chapter seven, the first Christians did not believe that this teaching office perished with the apostles, but continued to guide the Church in the bishops, the successors of the apostles. This allowed the Church to continually guide the faithful to salvation by declaring that certain doctrines are essential to the Faith, and that denying these doctrines is a grave sin that risks a person's eternal soul.

I want to be clear, though, that not everything the pope says or even that the Catholic Church teaches is an essential belief, "which must be believed with divine and catholic faith," whose denial results in the grave sin of heresy. A heretic isn't a baptized person who merely makes a gaffe or a theological error, but someone who doubles down and refuses to be corrected (obstinate denial). In addition, to be a heretic, one must deny a doctrine that the Catholic Church has *infallibly defined* as being part of divine revelation, or a dogma of the Faith.

For example, the Church infallibly teaches that human beings have immortal souls, so obstinately denying this truth would make one a heretic. The Church also teaches, but not in an infallible way, that God immediately creates our souls when we are conceived (CCC 306). Many Protestants agree with this non-infallible teaching, but some Protestant theologians say our souls come from our parents—a view called *traducianism*. The Catholic Church rejects traducianism through authoritative teaching, but it has not yet issued an infallible judgment on the matter.

Most Protestants would agree that non-essential Christian doctrines (what they might call secondary doctrines) are still important, and so they should not be treated in a flippant way. This is why Catholics are still obliged to obey non-infallible Church teachings even if denying these teachings doesn't constitute the grave sin of heresy. But Protestants have a difficult time explaining in a non-arbitrary way which biblical teachings fall under the scope of theological opinion, secondary doctrines, and primary or essential doctrines. In contrast, the Catholic Church can authoritatively teach that a doctrine is "essential" or a dogma through mechanisms like the decrees of an ecumenical council or the pope's solemn, "*ex cathedra*" statement. (For more on that see my colleague Jimmy Akin's aptly titled book *Teaching with Authority*.)

Catholic When It's (Historically) Convenient?

Only a small portion of the Church's doctrine involves teachings that it is the grave sin of heresy to deny. These are the doctrines make up the foundations of our faith. For example, at the fifth-century Council of Ephesus, the

Church infallibly taught that "Mary is the Mother of God" to refute the Nestorian heresy that the baby in Mary's womb was just the "human Christ" and not the Word made flesh described in John 1:14. The Church has issued condemnations of heresies like this at important points in history to save souls from joining sects that reject the fundamentals of the Faith.

But in response to the claim that Protestantism radically under-defines doctrine, leaving anything "up for grabs," some Protestants say Catholicism "over-defines" doctrine by obliging belief for doctrines that are, in their view, not well evidenced. They might say it is absurd for a person's salvation to depend on whether he rejects the dogma that Mary was assumed body and soul into heaven. But aside from the evidence we do have for this dogma, this objection relies on just an emotional reaction to a valid way of defining dogma.

The objector has simply picked a dogma that doesn't look like other dogmas that are more prominent in the biblical and historical record (e.g., Mary as the God-bearer). But that's like when a pro-choice person says biological species markers can't determine humanity because that would mean "an embryo is a human being." So? A human embryo may not look like other born human beings like you and me, but it fits the criteria of being human, and the objector hasn't proposed other criteria that more sensibly answers the question, "What is a human being?"

Likewise, a Protestant merely objecting to the Church's ability to define doctrine because he disagrees with some of the doctrines the Church has defined doesn't resolve the issue. He has no alternative criteria to offer to determine which doctrines are essential, about which debate among Christians must be brought to an end, and which are still debatable and have not reached their final, fully defined forms. (I am amused when Protestants who complain about the first Christian references to Mary's assumption coming hundreds of years after the Crucifixion demand that believers hold to a particular arrangement of the books of the Bible—also called the canon of Scripture—that was not referenced until hundreds of years after the Crucifixion.)

There is one point where my Supreme Court analogy breaks down, but not in Protestantism's favor. I can know the textual makeup of the U.S. Constitution apart from the Supreme Court's authority to interpret it. But how do Protestants know that the twenty-seven books of the New Testament constitute divine revelation that fulfills and surpasses the Old Testament?

There is no test we can apply to these documents to prove they are Scripture. For example, we can't say Scripture comprises just apostolic writings, because Mark and Luke weren't apostles. Most honest Protestants accept that God used the fourth-century Church and its regional councils' teachings on the canon of Scripture (namely, Hippo and Carthage in 382) to help future believers know which books belong in the Bible. But many Protestants say that during this time period, after Christianity became the official religion of the Roman Empire, the Church embraced many false doctrines, like the perpetual virginity of Mary, the Eucharist being the true body and blood of Christ, purgatory, the papacy, and many others. To which I ask these Protestants:

If the fourth-century Church got so many doctrines wrong, how do you know it got the canon of Scripture right? And if you do trust the Catholic Church on the question of what the Bible is, then why don't you trust the Catholic Church on the question of what the Bible teaches?

Under Protestantism, the "church" is a cacophony of contradictory voices united in the invisible bond of a vague "mere

Christianity" that rests on Christ's divinity but doesn't go into detail about what that doctrine means. It doesn't help to add the ecumenical councils to that discord of doctrine because some doctrines, like the existence of hell, original sin, and the male/female elements of marriage, weren't discussed at the early ecumenical councils . . . but they are still essential to the Faith.

Also, it is inconsistent to rely on these early councils as a standard of orthodoxy and ignore the Catholic elements within them. For example, the Council of Chalcedon defined the dogma of Christ's full humanity and divinity, but when a letter from Pope Leo was read there, all the bishops in attendance shouted, "Peter has spoken through Leo!"[6]

So, in order to remain united to Christ and his church, one cannot be an obstinate heretic. But Protestantism has no way to determine when permissible doctrinal disagreement becomes impermissible heresy. Fortunately, you don't have to be an expert in interpreting the Bible or be really good at picking the best theologian to follow to see if you are a heretic. The *Catechism* systematically presents what the Church teaches. By listening to Christ's Church, including its living voice that can answer novel theological questions, we can avoid the sin of heresy and remain faithful to the revelation God has given us.

This doesn't just include believing the right doctrines. It includes following right behavior. Our salvation depends not just on what we believe, but on how we put our belief into action: what we do and don't do. That's why John 3:36 says, "He who believes in the Son has eternal life; he who does not obey the Son shall not see life, but the wrath of God rests upon him."

Salvation comes through the Catholic Church because it teaches us which acts involve holy obedience to God's moral law and which involve sinful disobedience, which is incompatible with being a saved Christian.

CHAPTER 2

Right *Conduct*

The Catholic Church teaches us what actions are gravely sinful and must be avoided so we do not forsake our salvation.

Once, I was talking with a poised young Protestant woman who was adept at citing the Bible. The topic of James 2 and its insistence that a man is not justified by "faith alone" (which we'll discuss in chapter twenty) came up, to which she quickly responded,

"Of course, we are saved by faith alone. But true faith is never alone. Saving faith in Christ is always accompanied by good works. The works aren't what save us, but their presence shows that we are truly saved. They are the fruit of salvation."

I decided to take a break from trading Bible verses back and forth (which can often distract from a conversation's main purpose) and ask her some basic questions:

"What good works?"

"Excuse me?" she asked with a confused look on her face.

"You said that good works don't save us, but they are a sign that we are saved."

"Right."

"And if we don't have those good works in our life, that means we aren't saved?"

"Yeah. The works don't save us, but they are a sign that we are saved," she said.

"But then it sounds as though I really need to know what those works are, because what if I don't have them? Then I don't have the signs of salvation in my life, which would mean I'm not saved."

We talked a bit more, and she said that things like "feeding the homeless" are the good works that show that one has "saving faith."

"So, if I don't feed the homeless, I'll go to hell?"

She assured me, "No, no, no. I mean, there's lots of good works you can do to show you're saved. It's up to you to follow the Spirit on which ones God is calling you to do."

"Okay. So, if God is calling me to provide free abortions for the poor, should I listen and do that good work?"

"Absolutely not. That's the devil talking, not God."

As our conversation progressed, we found a piece of common ground: a truly saved person will live a certain way. As we saw from the previous chapter, this person will believe the essential teachings of the Christian faith, which we've seen Protestantism has a hard time articulating. And what makes this more difficult for Protestantism is that many of these essential beliefs aren't just theological in nature; they're moral. They are beliefs about which acts are saintly and which are sinful.

Catholics and Protestants agree about some manifestly sinful acts, like adultery and murder. We agree that these are incompatible with the Christian life. Although someone in friendship with God, such as King David, might fall into these sins, a truly saved person won't habitually engage in them.

But in my conversations with Protestants, I've found that many of them have grossly ignorant beliefs about gravely sinful acts. Without a universal teaching authority like the

Catholic Church, they end up rationalizing all kinds of sins under the guise of *sola scriptura*.

The Bible *Doesn't* Tell Me So?

"I mean, the Bible never says masturbation is always wrong."

I'd be surprised to hear any Christian say this, but I was aghast to hear a youth pastor from a nearby Protestant community tell me this in such a matter-of-fact way.

We were having what was supposed to be a casual "guys' night" involving local Christian men, both Catholic and Protestant. We talked about what teens in our respective youth programs were struggling with, and whereas we all agreed that pornography and lusting after people are sinful, I was shocked to see some of these men carve out an exception for the sin of masturbation.

"I mean, if it were possible to engage in self-stimulation to relieve sexual passions without having lustful thoughts, then I don't think that would be wrong, because the Bible never says that act is wrong—only the lustful desires."

It isn't just random youth pastors saying this kind of stuff. In one episode of my podcast, *The Counsel of Trent*, I showed clips of nearly half a dozen prominent Evangelical leaders making similar claims. James Dobson, the founder of Focus on the Family, once said, "It is my opinion that masturbation is not much of an issue with God. . . . You should not struggle with guilt over it." Conservative Protestant scholar Craig Blomberg says that for people who cannot marry and experience sexual frustration, "a limited use of masturbation would appear to be the most appropriate answer."[7]

The Catholic view of this issue strikes a balance between sinful permissiveness and unmerciful rigorism. One the one hand, the Church recognizes that our sexuality is a blessing from God meant to express a full gift of self to one's spouse. That why the *Catechism* says that to use our sexual powers toward a purely self-centered end is "an intrinsically and gravely disordered action." On the other hand, the Church recognizes that there are circumstances like "immaturity [i.e., being a very young person], force of acquired habit, conditions of anxiety, or other psychological or social factors that lessen, if not even reduce to a minimum, moral culpability" for this act (2352).

Now, a Protestant might say that he's heard Catholic priests offer carve-outs for masturbation. I wouldn't be surprised if some priests have failed to uphold the Faith. But the difference is that Catholicism has a universally adopted teaching on these matters that a wayward priest can be said to contradict, whereas for many Protestants, no such universal teaching authority exists.

One of the ways that salvation comes from the Catholic Church is that the Church provides believers with moral clarity so they can know which actions are compatible with the Christian life and which are not. Protestants may claim that the Holy Spirit or the plain meaning of Scripture will do this for believers, but experience shows that this is not the case.

For example, a Christian may believe that Evangelicalism or "non-denominationalism" is not an authentic representation of the historic Christian tradition, but he may still be skeptical of the Catholic Church. So, he might decide to become a Lutheran, a Presbyterian, or an Anglican. But be careful about which mainline Protestant denomination you choose. In America, the largest Lutheran body, the Evangelical Lutheran Church of America, supports so-called same-sex marriage. The same is true of several prominent Presbyterian, Methodist, and Anglican communities that have split over moral issues like homosexuality.

This is why Michael Coren, the author of the 2012 book *Why Catholics Are Right*, left the Catholic Church and became an Anglican priest in 2017. He once was a staunch defender of Christian morality, but now he endorses evils like sodomy, counterfeit "same-sex marriage," and abortion. He knows that the Catholic Church uniformly condemns these evils, so he chose to become a minister in a sufficiently liberal Anglican group that would accommodate his views.

This isn't just a problem with modern Protestant denominations. Even the Protestant Reformers had a difficult time grounding traditional moral codes in the framework of the Bible alone. Martin Luther didn't like polygamy, but he admitted that "if a man wishes to marry several wives, I cannot forbid it, nor is it in opposition to the holy scriptures."[8]

Luther even preferred bigamy to divorce, though he allowed divorce after remarriage in some cases in spite of this contradicting Christ's teaching that "whoever divorces his wife and marries another, commits adultery against her" (Mark 10:11). Other Reformers like Ulrich Zwingli and Martin Bucer went farther, allowing for remarriage under many conditions, including "mutual consent"—a prelude to today's "no-fault divorce."

There are some groups that call themselves Catholic and endorse grave moral evils, like the so-called "Old Catholic Church." These groups are not in communion with the real Catholic Church, and anyway, they make up 0.001 percent of those who call themselves Catholic. But even the most liberal Catholic parishes (i.e., the ones in communion with the pope) will not celebrate same-sex weddings or ordain female priests. They can't, because the Church has a "Catholic hierarchy," which comes from the Greek words for "universal" (*kata-holos*, "by the whole") and "sacred order" (*hieros archos*). The Church Jesus Christ established is able to implement a universal, sacred order to guide people across time and space to final salvation in him.

The Gift of the Magisterium

Some Protestants say they can identify which Protestant churches have adhered to longstanding Christian tradition, and so they don't need the Catholic Church's guidance. They think their preferred conservative denomination would never depart from the Church's 2,000-year-long witness on a matter of grave evil related to sexuality. What they don't know is that their denomination probably has done this in the past and still does this in the present.

In 1930, Pope Pius XI reaffirmed the Church's opposition to contraception and abortion in his encyclical *Casti Connubii*. Except for the Anglicans in that same year, no Protestant denomination made a statement against abortion until the 1960s. And even when they did, they often held a pro-choice position. The 1968 American Baptist Convention declared, "Because Christ calls us to affirm the freedom of persons and the sanctity of life, we recognize that abortion should be a matter of responsible personal decision." W.A. Criswell, a former president of the Southern Baptist Convention, said, "I have always felt that it was only after a child was born and had a life separate from its mother that it became an individual person, and it has always, therefore, seemed to me that what is best for the mother and for the future should be allowed." In 1976, *Christianity Today* asked the question "Is Abortion a Catholic Issue?," and even the legendary Billy Graham allowed for abortion in the case of rape or incest.[9] Sociologist Sabrina Danielsen has catalogued similar statements made by Lutherans, Presbyterians, the Church of Christ, and many other denominations.

All of this was rooted in the claim that because Scripture is not "clear" on abortion or when human life begins (aside from poetic passages in psalms or unique cases like the prenatal John the Baptist and Jesus), the Church cannot prohibit abortion.

But if we are obliged to follow the unanimous Christian condemnation of abortion prior to the 1960s, then aren't we obliged to follow the unanimous Christian condemnation of contraception during this period? Prior to 1930, all Christian denominations believed that contraception was sinful. Today, the Catholic Church is the only major denomination to hold this view. If Protestants believe that inherently sterile sex between people of the same sex is wrong and that this universal traditional view in the Church should be retained, then why don't they believe the same about purposefully sterile sex between a husband and wife?

In response, conservative Protestants might say that Scripture is sufficient to show them that abortion and homosexual acts are sinful, but Scripture is not as clear about contraception, so there is no inconsistency if they rely on Scripture alone, apart from the Church's Tradition.

First, Scripture might not be as perspicuous on abortion and homosexuality as these Protestants think. Many conservative denominations have succumbed to faulty revisionist theology that claims that the Bible condemns only pederasty between men and boys, or sexual exploitation between masters and slaves, not so-called "consensual same-sex relationships," which they (wrongly) claim were unknown in biblical times. Even Richard Hays, a conservative scholar whose work was used to defend the traditional teaching on homosexuality, has publicly changed his mind on this issue and endorses same-sex relationships.[10] Indeed, if almost the entire Protestant world could change its mind on the sin of contraception in less than one hundred years, who's to say it can't do the same on other issues of sexual morality?

Second, this response assumes that a thoughtful Protestant will always be able to apply the Bible to discern answers to ethical questions. But what about questions the biblical authors could not have imagined even in their worst nightmares?

Consider all the evils involved in *in vitro* fertilization. The husband often supplies sperm through masturbation, and then a child is created by combining it with the wife's ovum in a Petri dish. A lab tech, not the child's father, then technically impregnates the wife—unless the couple decides to rent another woman's womb to bring the child to term (a gestational surrogate). And that's assuming the couple is married. Why can't an unmarried woman use a sperm donor? Or an unmarried man use an egg donor? Technically, a man could hire out a sperm donor, egg donor, and gestational surrogate and have a child delivered to him nine months later.

Many Protestants who correctly adduce the wrongness of ripping a child from his mother's womb through abortion fail to see the wrongness of creating a child apart from his mother's womb and then placing him in the uterus of a stranger hired to carry him for nine months in a mercenary perversion of motherhood. Or if they do see that this is gravely evil, they struggle to show how the Bible mandates that all Christians should agree with them that this is incompatible with authentic Christianity.

This is why I'm grateful for the Church's authority on these matters. This includes speaking forcefully to the world and calling it back from the edge of moral madness, like when Pope Francis called for a global ban on surrogacy.[11] It also includes speaking forcefully *to me*, by pointing out what actions place my soul in danger, even if the Bible doesn't clearly condemn those acts, and I've tried to rationalize my own disordered love for them.

The Church provides similar guidance to what the evangelist Philip gave the Ethiopian eunuch who was reading Isaiah 53, the famous passage that speaks of the Messiah as the "suffering servant." Philip asks the eunuch if he understands what he is reading, to which the eunuch responds, "How can I, unless some one guides me?" (Acts 8:30–31). Philip then explains the scriptures and the gospel to the eunuch before baptizing him.

The Not So "Orthodox" Church

Up to this point, you may be wondering why salvation is from the Catholic Church and not also from the Eastern Orthodox churches, whose split from the Catholic Church is usually dated to the eleventh century, in an event called the Great Schism. Even though Catholic and Orthodox share much more theologically with each other than either does with Protestants, on these moral issues, even the Orthodox churches have departed from the most ancient understanding of the Faith.

For example, the early Church did not agree with Roman laws that allowed remarriage after divorce. In his defense of the Church written to the Roman emperor, Justin Martyr made this clear by quoting Jesus' prohibition on remarriage after divorce and then saying, "All who, by human law, are twice married, are in the eye of our Master sinners."[12] A. Andrew Das's comprehensive treatment of marriage and divorce in the early Church puts it this way: "To marry a woman after divorce is to commit adultery. The ante-Nicene [pre-A.D. 325] authors simply never countenance any party of divorce—whether innocent or not, whether the divorce was legitimate or not—marrying again unless the former spouse has died."[13]

After Nicaea, some Church Fathers, like St. Basil, inconsistently allowed remarriage after divorce, such as for a husband who was the victim of an adulterous spouse but not a wife in the same position.[14] Later authors of Eastern canon law (the law of the Church) adopted the "pro-divorce" canons of the Byzantine emperor Julian on the matter. But even many Eastern Christians, like John Chrysostom, opposed this practice. He said, "Both by the manner of the creation, and by the manner of lawgiving, [Jesus] showed that one man must dwell with one woman continually, and never break off from her."[15]

The modern Eastern Orthodox churches do not hold to these more ancient views, as can be seen in the Orthodox Church of America (OCA)'s website, which says that the OCA "does permit divorced individuals to marry a second and even a third time."[16] In contrast, the *Catechism* says that "divorce does injury to the covenant of salvation, of which sacramental marriage is the sign. Contracting a new union, even if it is recognized by civil law, adds to the gravity of the rupture: the remarried spouse is then in a situation of public adultery" (2384).

Some people claim that Catholics permit remarriage after divorce, as the Orthodox do, but they call it an "annulment" instead. However, unlike divorce, which attempts to dissolve a valid marriage, a declaration of nullity (an "annulment") says there was never a valid marriage in the first place. It only appeared as though the couple were married on their wedding day, but a necessary element of marriage was missing. There may have been impediments, like fraud, coercion, or an inability to fully consent, that kept the marital union from coming into being. Annulments, many of which are not granted, are concerned with how the marriage began, in order to ascertain whether a marriage truly began at all. Divorce, on the other hand, tries to end a valid marriage—but

Jesus solemnly declares, "What God has joined let not man put asunder."

The Orthodox have also loosened their once-firm moral stance against contraceptives. Orthodox scholar Tikhon Alexander Pino summarizes his church's evolution of thought on the issue:

> As contraception has become normalized in society at large, so it has become ordinary and accepted within the Orthodox Church. . . . The gradual and palpable shift is famously on display in successive editions of *The Orthodox Church* by Metropolitan Kallistos Ware. Writing in 1963, as Timothy Ware, the future metropolitan stated unequivocally that "artificial methods of birth control are forbidden in the Orthodox Church."
>
> Twenty years later, this statement would be adjusted to account for changes that were then in the air: "Some bishops and theologians altogether condemn the employment of [artificial methods of birth control]. Others, however, have recently begun to adopt a less strict position." A decade later, Bishop Kallistos narrates the end of the process: "In the past birth control was in general strongly condemned, but today a less strict view is coming to prevail."[17]

Pino admits there has not been a universal teaching on contraception among the Orthodox on par with something like Catholic encyclicals or the Church's universal catechism. Renowned Orthodox scholar John Meyendorff says, "The Orthodox Church, for its part, has never committed itself formally and officially on this issue."[18]

This has led to variation among Orthodox churches on this issue, with a fair amount of laxity among them. For example, the Russian Orthodox Church's *Basis of the Social Concept* distinguishes "abortive" and "non-abortive" contraception and criticizes the latter only if it involves "deliberate refusal of childbirth on egoistic grounds." The Orthodox Church in America likewise teaches that "only those means of controlling conception within marriage are acceptable which do not harm a fetus already conceived."[19]

Throughout history, there have been many Orthodox churches who longed to be in complete union with the successor of St. Peter. They became Catholic churches that retain Eastern modes of worship and cultural practices (e.g., having an Eastern calendar of fasting and holy days, which differs from the Western Church's). The Catholic Church seeks reunion with all the Eastern Orthodox because we share the same view on the role of priestly authority and the nature of the sacraments, like the Eucharist.

Such union with Protestant denominations would be a much taller order. This is because they have neglected God's revelation about one of the most important things we must do to be saved: eat the flesh and blood of our Savior, Jesus Christ.

CHAPTER 3

Right *Eucharist*

The Catholic Church gives us the true body and blood of Jesus Christ.

Once, when speaking with a Protestant friend about the age of the earth, I told him Genesis could be symbolically describing God's Creation over a long period of time, not literally describing a week that happened a few thousand years ago. He told me, "It says on the first day: morning and evening. Then 'the second day.' I don't know how you can get clearer than that. Why would I think this is just a symbol?"

I decided to be a little cheeky and flipped to Jesus' teaching about the "Bread of Life" in John 6. I asked my friend to read the part where Jesus says this:

> Truly, truly, I say to you, unless you eat the flesh of the Son of Man and drink his blood, you have no life in you; he who eats my flesh and drinks my blood has eternal life, and I will raise him up at the last day. For my flesh is food indeed, and my blood is drink indeed.
>
> He who eats my flesh and drinks my blood abides in me, and I in him. As the living Father sent me, and I live because of the Father, so he who eats me will live because of me (John 6:53–57)

He closed the Bible and simply said in response, "That's symbolic."

Wait! What happened to "How much clearer can you get?"

My friend's appeal to "symbolic language" here was not only very convenient, but also flat-out nonsensical. As I'll show, saying the Eucharist is merely a symbol of Christ, as opposed to Christ himself, raises more questions than it answers. It also shows why salvation comes from the Church, which has safeguarded 2,000 years of tradition regarding the Lord's real presence in "the Lord's Supper."

Symbolic Senselessness

Why is belief in the real presence of Christ in the Eucharist required for our salvation? Because Jesus Christ said that if we don't eat his flesh and drink his blood, we won't have eternal life. That's a good enough answer for me! If anything counts as "believing in Jesus" for our salvation, then shouldn't that include believing in what Jesus said about his presence in the Eucharist?

Some Protestants say "eating Jesus' flesh" and "drinking his blood" are merely metaphors to refer to having faith in him. The problem with that explanation is that Jesus *does* speak symbolically about food in John's Gospel, just a few chapters earlier, and he corrects the disciples when they misunderstand him. He says, "My food is to do the will of him who sent me, and to accomplish his work" (John 4:34). But in John 6:66, we learn that "after this many of his disciples drew back and no longer went about with him." Jesus does not correct them, because he wasn't proposing a symbol they misunderstood; he was offering the gift of himself, in bread and wine, that they rejected.

Jesus also said, "It is the spirit that gives life, the flesh is of no avail" (John 6:63) not because the Eucharist is merely a symbol. (He didn't say, "*My* flesh is of no avail.") Jesus said this because his disciples still doubted that he could give them his body as food. They were stuck in man-focused "fleshy" ways, as opposed to spiritual ways of thinking that recognize God's almighty power. The latter way of thinking would have allowed them to trust Jesus when he said, "The words that I have spoken to you are spirit and life."

Another reason to believe that Jesus' words were not symbols is that the phrase "eating my flesh" was symbolic . . . of cursing someone (Mic. 3:1-3). And even if Jesus didn't mind that he was echoing cursing language to symbolize spiritual nourishment that comes from belief in him, why did he talk about drinking *blood*? There are a thousand better forms of nourishment Jesus could have used to make a merely symbolic point . . . especially since drinking blood had been forbidden since the time of Genesis (9:4).

Through the Eucharist given to us at every Mass, we receive the risen, glorified new Passover sacrifice, whose death takes away the sins of the world. We receive him in a miraculous, unbloody way, under the form of bread and wine.

The early Christians were clear that these elements of the Mass are not merely bread and wine that serve as reminders of what Christ did for us. St. Ignatius of Antioch, who calls the Eucharist "the medicine of immortality," said that heretics "confess not the Eucharist to be the flesh of our Savior Jesus Christ, which suffered for our sins, and which the Father, of his goodness, raised up again."[20] Justin Martyr said the Eucharistic Prayer at Mass changes the bread and wine so that they become "the flesh and blood of that Jesus who was made flesh."[21] The Protestant scholar Darwell Stone said, "Throughout the writings of the Fathers there is unbroken agreement that the consecrated bread and wine are the body and blood of Christ, and that the Eucharist is a sacrifice."[22]

Looks Can Be Deceiving

Paul said that he who "eats the bread or drinks the cup of the Lord in an unworthy manner will be guilty of profaning the body and blood of the Lord" (1 Cor. 11:27). A failure to treat the Eucharist with the reverence due was such a serious evil that it resulted in many members of the Corinthian church falling ill or even dying. If someone tears up a picture of my family, I may be offended, but I would never say he violated my family members' bodies. But such a judgment makes sense if the Eucharist is not merely an *image* of Christ but *is* Christ himself.

"But it still looks like bread and wine," you might say.

And Jesus looked like any other first-century craftsman. Isaiah even says he had "no beauty that we should desire him" (Isa. 53:2). Jesus didn't "look like God" because Jesus' divine properties could be "seen" only through the testimonies about him and his miracles. Likewise, the bread and wine at Mass look like ordinary bread and wine, but Jesus said they are not merely those appearances. Jesus did not say at the Last Supper, "This bread contains my body" or "My blood is with this wine." He said this *is* my body, and this *is* my blood of the New Covenant.

Catholics have developed the language of *form* and *substance* to describe what happens at Mass when the form of bread and wine remain, but their substance becomes the body and blood of Christ. For example, the form of my body changes over time. After I was conceived, it was only the size of a single cell. But the substance who I am, Trent Horn, was the same from conception until the moment I wrote these words. It is not identical to any physical collection, since my body doesn't have the same cells I once had as an embryo. This substance is the "metaphysical core" that gives me my identity and unites my changing appearances.

Human beings can change a thing's form, but we can't change a thing's substance without causing it to stop existing. You can cut my hair, and I'd still be Trent Horn, but if you kept cutting and took my head off, I wouldn't be "Trent Horn" anymore; I'd be Trent Horn's corpse. But through his omnipotent power over creation, God is able to cause the bread and wine at Mass to retain their appearance (their form) while changing their substance into Christ's body and blood for us to receive as the new Passover sacrifice that takes away the sins of the world.

One Sacrifice

The Passover lamb in the Old Testament had to be a male, without blemish, and his legs could not be broken. Christ, our Passover lamb, is male. According to Hebrews 4:15, he is without sin. And as John 19:33 describes it, his legs were not broken during the Crucifixion. Finally, the Passover was not complete until the lamb was eaten, and so the "Passover" that Christians still celebrate must be completed in a similar way. The *Catechism* says that the Eucharist was instituted at the Last Supper "in order to perpetuate the sacrifice of the cross throughout the ages until he should come again" (1323). It adds,

> The sacrifice of Christ and the sacrifice of the Eucharist are *one single sacrifice*. . . . "In this divine sacrifice which is celebrated in the Mass, the same Christ who offered himself once in a bloody manner on the altar of the cross is contained and is offered in an unbloody manner. . . . This sacrifice is truly propitiatory" (1367).

Protestants claim that describing the Mass as a sacrifice contradicts Scripture's testimony that Christ's death on the cross was the one and *only* sacrifice that atones for our sins.

Hebrews 10:10 says, "We have been sanctified through the offering of the body of Jesus Christ once for all." The letter to the Hebrews is clear that, unlike the animal sacrifices of the Old Testament, Christ's sacrifice was perfect and does not need to be repeated continually. Christ is not sacrificed anew at every Mass. Instead, Christ's one bloody sacrifice on the cross is re-presented to the Father for the atonement of sin under the unbloody form of bread and wine.

The importance of gathering to offer this sacrifice and to receive it can be seen in the earliest Church writings. The first-century author of the *Didache* advised Christians to "break bread and offer the Eucharist; but first make confession of your faults, so that your sacrifice may be a pure one." In the second century, Justin Martyr believed that the Eucharist fulfilled the prophecy of Malachi 1:11, that a pure offering would be made everywhere in the Lord's name. He said, "In every place offer sacrifices to him—i.e., the bread of the Eucharist, and also the cup of the Eucharist." In the third century, St. Cyprian of Carthage said,

> If Christ Jesus, our Lord and God, is himself the high priest of God the Father; and if he offered himself as a sacrifice to the Father; and if he commanded that this be done in commemoration of himself, then certainly the priest, who imitates that which Christ did, truly functions in place of Christ.

But didn't Jesus say to "do this," or offer the Eucharist, in "memory of me" (Luke 22:19)? How can the Eucharist be offered in memory of Christ if Christ is truly present in the Eucharist on the altar? The answer is that it is not you and I or any other human being doing the "remembering."

The Protestant scholar Joachim Jeremias has shown that the Greek word rendered "remembrance" in this passage (*anamnesin*) refers to more than just a purely spiritual recollection.[23] The same word occurs in Numbers 10:10, saying that this "shall serve you for remembrance [*anamnesis*] before your God." (The Hebrew original means the same thing.) Likewise, Hebrews 10:3 says, "In these sacrifices there is a reminder of sin year after year." In both cases, the sacrifices are not for human beings to remember what God has done, but for God to figuratively remember what human beings have done. In Luke 22:19, Jesus is literally saying, "This is my body, which is given for you. Offer this memorial sacrifice to God."

Which Church?

To be saved, we must be obedient to Christ. And Christ commands us to receive him in the Eucharist. But can we go to any church to receive Christ in the Eucharist? Or must we go to the one Church that Christ founded upon the apostles that will visibly and perpetually exist until Christ returns in glory?

Although some Evangelicals believe that the Eucharist is only a memorial symbol, and thus celebrate the Lord's Supper monthly or even every few months, other more traditional Protestant denominations celebrate the Lord's Supper each week and claim that they too believe in "the real presence" of Christ in the Eucharist.

Presbyterians and those who follow the Reformed theology of John Calvin say Christ is present in the bread and wine through the Holy Spirit, but this is true only for those who have faith when they receive the bread and wine. Lutherans have a view called *sacramental union* that goes farther, saying Christ is fully present in the bread and wine in the same way water is present in a sponge. Lutherans would say the bread and wine truly contain Christ's body and blood, and so receiving the Eucharist communicates the forgiveness of sins. And, unlike for Reformed Christians, Christ is present in the Eucharist even if the person receiving does not believe this about the Lord's Supper.

But what all Protestant denominations have in common is that they deny that the bread and wine *become* the body and blood of Jesus Christ. They do not, for example, encourage adoring the Eucharist as one would adore Christ in heaven. They also deny that what is offered in the Eucharist is the one sacrifice of Christ that takes away the sins of the world. Martin Luther even said of the Church Fathers who held this belief that "it would yet be the safer course to reject them all rather than admit that the Mass is a work or a sacrifice."[24]

Salvation comes from the Catholic Church because the Eucharist at Mass is not a symbol of Christ. It is not bread and wine that spiritually contain the body and blood of Christ. Instead, after the priest says the prayer of consecration, the bread and wine change, and all that remains on the altar is the body and blood of Jesus Christ under the form of bread and wine. This allows us to receive Christ's saving flesh and blood as the new Passover lamb, but it also allows us to offer God the highest form of worship, which is necessary for our salvation.

CHAPTER 4

Right *Worship*

The Catholic Church enables us to worship God properly.

One Sunday during my pro-life missionary days, I was heading to Mass with my Catholic teammates when I saw Kevin, one of our Protestant colleagues, sitting at the kitchen table in our host home, sipping coffee and reading his Bible.

"Do you want to go to Mass with us?" I asked.

"Nah, I'm good," he replied.

"So, I guess you're going to First Baptist Church instead?"

"No, I don't really go to church," he said, without any indication that what he said was a big deal. "I usually just stay home and read my Bible. Sometimes me and my friends do Bible studies, but the Bible never says you have to go to church."

It turns out Kevin was right.

I mean, he was wrong about our obligation as Christians to worship at church on Sunday, but he was right that this sacred obligation is not recorded in Scripture.[25] Although the Bible describes believers meeting in their homes to break bread (Acts 2:42–47), it never commands believers to attend church every Sunday. It also never commands us to celebrate important feasts like Christmas (which is why some Protestants don't).

Most Protestants at least believe that Christians have an obligation to join a local church and worship there on Sunday. But why do we have this obligation? Is it to help us grow spiritually? Is it to hear the word preached to us in a sermon? The answer to this question reveals one of the biggest differences between Catholics and Protestants as well as why salvation comes from the Catholic Church and not Protestant communities: we attend church on Sunday to fulfill our obligation to offer God on the Lord's Day our highest form of worship.

And Protestant churches do not offer God the *highest* form of worship.

What Is *Worship*?

If you are Protestant, your eyebrows may have shot to the top of your head after reading the previous sentence. You might be thinking:

What do you mean, "Protestants don't give God the highest form of worship?" Have you even been to a reverent Protestant Sunday service? How can you deny the movement of the Holy Spirit in the worship taking place?

To see what I mean, we need to define the word *worship*.

Worship comes from an old English word that means to give someone his "worth-ship"—to give a person what he is worth or due. Worship was given to God, but lesser forms of it could also be given to human beings based on their worths-ship. For example, the *Old English Prayer Book* instructs a groom to tell his bride on his wedding day, "With my body I thee worship." He gives his body to her because she is worth receiving that gift by virtue of being his wife. Even today, some countries refer to civil magistrates like judges as "your worship," and in the United States we call judges "your honor." The Protestant scholar D.A. Carson agrees that worship has changed in meaning over time, but historically, "in all such usages one is concerned with the 'worthiness' or the 'worthship' (Old English *weorthscipe*) of the person or thing that is reverenced."[26]

What, then, is God "worth," or worthy of receiving from us?

We might give God praise through a spoken prayer or a song that thanks, praises, or makes a petition to him. Psalm 145:3 says, "Great is the Lord and greatly to be praised; his greatness is unsearchable." God deserves our praise, but human beings also deserve praise when they do good things—just not the same degree of praise we give to God. The Blessed Virgin Mary said, "All generations will call me blessed; for he who is mighty has done great things for me, and holy is his name" (Luke 1:48-49).

Protestant worship takes good things we already do, like offering praise, and gives the best of those good things to God. Or as the title of Baptist author Oswald Chambers's 1924 devotional puts it: *My Utmost for His Highest.*

And don't get me wrong—this is good and holy. Colossians 3:16 says, "Let the word of Christ dwell in you richly, as you teach and admonish one another in all wisdom, and as you sing psalms and hymns and spiritual songs with thankfulness in your hearts to God." Our worship should give God praise and honor that is reserved for him alone. For example, we don't praise Mary for creating the universe, but we do praise God for that, as can be seen in Revelation 4:11, where the elders in heaven exclaim, "Worthy art thou, our Lord and God, to receive glory and honor and power, for thou didst create all things."

But Catholic and Orthodox liturgies give God not just the highest degree of goods we give to other creatures, like our highest praise, but the highest kind of thing we can give to God—specifically, sacrifice.

The Sanctity of Sacrifice

All cultures around the world recognize the deep desire in human beings to offer what they love as an act of love for God. These sacrifices might involve food; money; or, in more grim circumstances, human beings. Christianity teaches that all our worship is sacrificial in some way. Romans 12:1 says, "I appeal to you therefore, brethren, by the mercies of God, to present your bodies as a living sacrifice, holy and acceptable to God, which is your spiritual worship." Hebrews 13:15–16 says, "Let us continually offer up a sacrifice of praise to God, that is, the fruit of lips that acknowledge his name. Do not neglect to do good and to share what you have, for such sacrifices are pleasing to God."

However, in the Mass, or the Divine Liturgy as it's called in the East, the priest leads the faithful in worship that is not just of the highest degree. We don't give God the best of what creatures possess. Remember, worship means to give someone his "worth-ship," and God is infinite being itself. So, what is God worth?

There is only one thing we can give God that truly satisfies what God is worth as an offering to his majesty. We offer God the Father the exact same offering God the Son made to him in atonement for the sins of the world on the cross at Calvary. We give God what God gave us—himself—and that is the only thing we finite creatures can give that honors God's infinite worth.

Catholic theology is clear that whereas honor and respect can be given to Mary and the saints, sacrifice is a different, higher kind of worship, and this can be given only to God. That's why Christians in ancient Rome chose martyrdom over making an offering of incense to a false god. In the fourth century, St. Epiphanius condemned the Collyridian heretics, who offered sacrificial cakes to Mary, because sacrifice can only be given to God. St. Augustine said, "Putting aside for the present the other religious services with which God is worshiped, certainly no man would dare to say that sacrifice is due to any but God. . . . Who ever thought of sacrificing save to one whom he knew, supposed, or feigned to be a god?"[27]

The Mass is a sacrifice of praise and thanks, because we offer ourselves to God through our corporate worship, but it isn't just a sacrifice of praise. The *Catechism* says, "The Eucharist is also the sacrifice of praise by which the Church sings the glory of God in the name of all creation. This sacrifice of praise is possible only through Christ: he unites the faithful to his person, to his praise, and to his intercession, so that the sacrifice of praise to the Father is offered *through* Christ and *with* him, to be accepted *in* him" (1361).

The *Catechism* also calls the Eucharist the "source and summit" of our faith because it re-presents—not re-sacrifices, but re-presents—Christ's one perfect sacrifice under the form of bread and wine. It says,

> The Eucharist is the memorial of Christ's Passover, the making present and the sacramental offering of his unique sacrifice, in the liturgy of the Church which is his body. In all the eucharistic prayers we find after the words of institution a prayer called the *anamnesis* or memorial. In the sense of Sacred Scripture the memorial is not merely the recollection of past events but the proclamation of the mighty works wrought by God for men.
>
> In the liturgical celebration of these events, they become in a certain way present and real. This is how Israel understands its liberation from Egypt: every time Passover is celebrated, the Exodus events are made present

to the memory of believers so that they may conform their lives to them. In the New Testament, the memorial takes on new meaning. When the Church celebrates the Eucharist, she commemorates Christ's Passover, and it is made present the sacrifice Christ offered once for all on the cross remains ever present (1363-1364).

Sermon or Supper?

At many Protestant gatherings, the focal point of the service is not the Eucharist, or what they usually call the Lord's Supper. Instead, the focal point is the pastor's sermon. Attending church becomes focused on receiving God through the reading of his word and the teaching of his ministers. The Baptist author O.S. Hawkins puts it bluntly:

> The sermon is the central dynamic in the worship experience. It is the fulcrum upon which the entire service of worship hinges. Everything that comes before it should point to it, and everything that comes after it should issue out of it. Because of this, the pastor is the worship leader of the church.[28]

This is very different from how Catholics describe the celebration of the Eucharist. The *Catechism* says the Eucharist, the body and blood of Jesus Christ under the form of bread and wine, is the source and summit of our faith. That's why everything in the liturgy points toward or back not to the homily the priest gives, but to the person being offered on the altar: Jesus Christ.

In the second century, Justin Martyr described Christian worship. Though he makes a passing reference to how the presider "verbally instructs" after the readings, most of his explanation concerns the Eucharist. He writes,

> This food is called among us *Eucharistia* of which no one is allowed to partake but the man who believes that the things which we teach are true, and who has been washed with the washing that is for the remission of sins, and unto regeneration, and who is so living as Christ has enjoined.
>
> For not as common bread and common drink do we receive these; but in like manner as Jesus Christ our Savior, having been made flesh by the Word of God, had both flesh and blood for our salvation, so likewise have we been taught that the food which is blessed by the prayer of his word, and from which our blood and flesh by transmutation are nourished, is the flesh and blood of that Jesus who was made flesh.[29]

Protestant pastors might spend their whole week planning a blockbuster sermon for the Sunday service, and the increasing length of sermons is what caused churches in the fifteenth century to construct pews. That's right: for 1,400 years, Christians did not sit in pews at church. They would stand and bow because they were not there to listen to a sermon. They were there to actively take part in worshiping God through the sacrifice of the Eucharist offered on the altar. The author of Hebrews tells us to imitate the faith of our leaders and to remember that "we have an altar from which those who serve the tent [i.e., the Jewish priests] have no right to eat" (13:10).

Teaching about God is good, but this isn't the highest worship of God, because we teach about all kinds of things. Singing praise to God is good, but it isn't the highest worship of God, because we praise many of God's creatures. Singing praises that are unique to God ("You are almighty, Lord") also isn't the highest form of worship because we are just acknowledging unique truths about God. Even the demons believe these unique truths about God, though they tremble at them (James 2:19). Instead, for 2,000 years, the Church has taught that the highest form of worship we give to God is *sacrifice.* This is why Paul warned the Corinthians not to fall into idolatry—because what the pagans call "Zeus" was just a demon. He wrote,

> What pagans sacrifice they offer to demons and not to God. I do not want you to be partners with demons. You cannot drink the cup of the Lord and the cup of demons. You cannot partake of the table of the Lord and the table of demons. Shall we provoke the Lord to jealousy? Are we stronger than he? (1 Cor. 10:20-22).

The "table" in both cases refers to a sacrificial altar. Christians cannot offer sacrifices to demons and sacrifices to God. But this means the first Christians were offering sacrifices to God! They did not offer God bulls and goats, because those can't take away sin (Heb. 10:4). Instead, they offered Christ himself to God the Father in the form of bread and wine of the Eucharist. This is why Paul said, "The cup of blessing which we bless, is it not a participation in the blood of Christ? The bread which we break, is it not a participation in the body of Christ?" (1 Cor. 10:16).

Giving God God's Worth

Apostolic Christianity, which includes Catholics and the Eastern Orthodox, maintains the 2,000-year-old tradition of giving God true worship through a sacrifice that is worthy of his infinite majesty. Nothing we have comes anywhere close to having that value. Instead, we give God the only thing that has this value: God himself. In thanksgiving for his mercy

(*Eucharist* means "thanksgiving"), we re-present to God the sacrifice Christ made on the cross under the unbloody form of bread and wine.

In the first century, an ancient catechism called the *Didache* ("teaching of the Twelve") told Christians: let no one eat or drink of your Thanksgiving (Eucharist), but they who have been baptized into the name of the Lord; for concerning this also the Lord has said, "Do not give dogs what is holy" (Matt 7:6). That means that to obey God's command to receive him as the new Passover lamb, we must first be incorporated into God's new covenant.

I have met many Christians who have become convinced that Christ is, unlike in the Lord's Supper at their home church, really and truly present in the Eucharist at Mass. They eagerly desire to receive Christ's body and blood. But I remind them that when we receive what they call "communion" at Mass, this is a public declaration that we are in communion with Christ and his Church. When we say "amen" upon receiving the body of Christ, we are saying "amen" not just to the Church's teaching on Christ in the Eucharist, but to all the teachings that God has given us through divine revelation. This means that if someone is a Protestant, or even a Catholic in a state of grave sin, he cannot receive Communion before being brought back into communion with Christ's Church.

For Catholics, this means being reconciled through the sacrament of confession, which we'll talk about in chapter six. For other Christians, this means being sealed in the oil of confirmation, which makes one an adult in the Faith, and, if they have not already, being baptized. One cannot receive the Passover sacrifice of the New Covenant without formally belonging to that covenant. And whereas entry into the Old Covenant was through circumcision, this has been replaced in the New Covenant with baptism, what St. Paul calls the circumcision of Christ (Col. 2:11-12). In the next chapter, we will see how the Church saves us through this all-important sacrament.

CHAPTER 5

Right *Baptism*

The Catholic Church provides one baptism for the forgiveness of sins.

I was excited to find out that Tiffany wanted to become Christian, but I and several others at our high school always thought her boyfriend was . . . strange. One time, I drove up to a party they were attending, and her boyfriend was standing on the front lawn, just staring off into the distance. As I walked in, I asked him what he was doing. He responded with a strange, dead-eyed stare that refused to acknowledge me and said, while staring off into the void,

"Just taking in the scene, man. Just taking in the scene."

I nodded and quickly went inside, wondering what Tiffany saw in a guy who treated other people as accessories for his own amusement rather than . . . well, people.

A few weeks later, Tiffany told me about her decision to be baptized. I was thrilled, but I was still concerned that such an important event in her life would forever be tied to this guy (who, you won't be surprised, dumped Tiffany a few months later). In fact, she ended up being re-baptized into another church, because there was doubt about whether this baptism was even valid.

Nearly all Christians agree that baptism is something we ought to do because the Lord commanded it. But how exactly is baptism to be done? The Catholic Church provides the answer: the Church has the fullest expression of the Lord's teaching on baptism, in contrast to Protestants, who are divided on important questions related to the crucial "first step" in many people's salvation.

Why Baptism Is a Salvation Issue

In this book we are discussing what one must *do* to be saved. At first glance, it may not seem necessary to discuss baptism, since nearly all Christians believe in baptism. Catholics, Orthodox, and certain Protestants like Lutherans and Anglicans believe that baptism is what saves us from sin. Other Protestants say baptism is a sign that confirms that a person has saving faith. Baptism may still provide certain spiritual benefits, but it is not the method that God uses to spiritually regenerate our souls. That's why, in their denominations, baptism is given only to adults and older children who ask for it *after* coming to faith in Christ.

So, if all Christians get baptized, albeit for different reasons, then why even bother discussing our theological differences on the matter? The reason baptism cannot be ignored is that we don't "all" get baptized. Many Protestants who reject baptismal regeneration also reject infant baptism. But if baptism is what saves us, then untold numbers of human beings are denied the ordinary means God gave us to secure their salvation.

Another important reason to talk about baptism is that if someone denies the doctrine of baptismal regeneration, then he's more likely to succumb to the "born-again argument" common among Evangelicals. They say that the only way to be saved is not to do good deeds or attend church; it's to be "born again." What does that mean? Usually, an act of declaring Jesus Christ as their Lord and Savior or putting faith in him in some similar way.

Like all errors, there is some truth mixed into the "born-again argument."

Merely attending church or doing good deeds is not what saves us. Becoming a child of God is what saves us, and we cannot be children of God if we reject having faith in God the Father, Son, and Holy Spirit. However, we are not "born again" at the first moment we have this experience of faith. This experience is a work of the Holy Spirit, but it is not the moment we receive the Holy Spirit and our souls are filled with God's sanctifying grace.

Thinking otherwise—that being "born again" is a matter of personal conviction or declaration—can lead to anxiously wondering if you were "really saved in the first place" or if you had a "true faith" rather than a false faith. I've known countless Protestants who told me about how they thought they were saved in elementary or middle school, only to realize they didn't make the "right act of faith" until later in life.

That's why we should not make the first moment we had faith (which isn't easy to locate, given the gradual nature of conversions) the "anchor point" for our salvation that gives us assurance. God has given us another, more stable and visible foundation of the beginning of our life in him: the waters of baptism.

Truly Born Again and Saved from Sin

Our Lord told Nicodemus in John 3:5 that "unless one is born of water and the Spirit, he cannot enter the kingdom of God." Many Protestants have tried to interpret the "water" in this passage as something other than the waters of baptism. One common alternative is the waters of the womb. The idea is that one must be born twice—once in a natural way, through "water" (natural birth), and then again in a spiritual way, through faith. But the Bible never refers to natural birth as the process of being "born of water." Instead, it uses phrases like "born of the flesh," as can be seen in the next verse, where Jesus says, "That which is born of the flesh is flesh, and that which is born of the Spirit is spirit" (John 3:6).

Every Church Father who cited this prior to the Council of Nicaea believed that John 3:5 is talking about Christian baptism. In the second century, Justin Martyr said, "In the name of God, the Father and Lord of the universe, and of our Savior Jesus Christ, and of the Holy Spirit, they then receive the washing with water. For Christ also said, 'Unless you be born again, you shall not enter into the kingdom of heaven.'"[30]

That doesn't mean a person never has to develop faith in Christ after baptism. Rather, baptism is what gives us God's grace and a corresponding spiritual disposition to have faith in Christ that works through love toward him. In the first sermon given after Pentecost, St. Peter told a crowd in Jerusalem that God had raised Jesus of Nazareth from the dead and that "God has made him both Lord and Christ, this Jesus whom you crucified" (Acts 2:36). Luke tells us that when the crowd heard this, "they were cut to the heart, and said to Peter and the rest of the apostles, 'Brethren, what shall we do?'" Peter replied,

> Repent, and be baptized every one of you in the name of Jesus Christ for the forgiveness of your sins; and you shall receive the gift of the Holy Spirit. For the promise is to you and to your children and to all that are far off, every one whom the Lord our God calls to him (Acts 2:38–39).

Some Protestants say that this shows people being baptized only because they have already been forgiven of their sins, not in order to receive the forgiveness of sins. But this makes the grammar of the passage very awkward, and it still doesn't explain the motivation of everyone in the narrative. The crowd were "cut to the heart" and feared divine judgment. They were seeking a means to be forgiven, and Peter gave it to them: through baptism. That Peter meant this can be seen in his own letter in the Bible, where he literally says that baptism saves us:

> In the days of Noah, during the building of the ark . . . a few, that is, eight persons, were saved through water. Baptism, which corresponds to this, now saves you, not as a removal of dirt from the body but as an appeal to God for a clear conscience, through the resurrection of Jesus Christ (1 Pet. 3:20-21).

The Water that Saves

Protestants who deny baptismal regeneration say Peter is just saying baptism is the way we show others we have been saved, and what really saves us is our appeal to God for a clean conscience, not liquid water. But Peter explicitly says those on Noah's ark were saved *through water.* Peter's point is that the liquid water itself doesn't magically save us or make us clean by taking away dirt. Instead, *seeking baptism* is the way we appeal to God for a clean conscience. Protestant scholar Oscar Cullmann says, "Just as ordinary water takes away the physical uncleanness of the body, so the water of baptism will take away sins."[31]

We also see in the conversion of St. Paul how baptism is used to cleanse people of sin and give them supernatural life. After encountering Jesus on the road to Damascus, Paul is struck blind and is taken in by a Christian named Ananias, who was sent by Jesus to restore Paul's sight. After laying hands on him, he tells Paul, "Why do you wait? Rise and be baptized, and wash away your sins, calling on his name" (Acts 22:16).

Some Protestants say Paul had already been saved before this point because he called Jesus "Lord" when he encountered him on the road. However, in the Bible, there are people who refer to Jesus as Lord (in Greek, *kurios*), with no indication that they believed he was the Messiah, much less God incarnate. In John 4:11, the woman at the well calls Jesus *kurios*. Most English translations render the word "sir"; the same translation can be found in the Pharisees who call Pontius Pilate *kurios* in Matthew 27:63. This was a title of respect in the ancient world that did not always refer to God.

That Paul believed that baptism saved him and us can be seen in his letter to Titus, where he says God "saved us, not because of deeds done by us in righteousness, but in virtue of his own mercy, by the washing of regeneration and renewal in the Holy Spirit" (3:5).

Some Protestants say baptism can't be what saves us because baptism is a work, and no work can lead to our initial salvation, which is by grace alone (Eph. 2:8–9). True, but that proves only that baptism isn't a *work*. Martin Luther said something similar: "Yes, our works, indeed, avail nothing for salvation; baptism, however, is not our work, but God's."[32]

So, when someone asks me if I have been "born again," I tell him, "Amen, I have! I was born again the moment I was baptized as a teenager, and my wife was born again once the waters of baptism fell upon her as an infant."

What About Infants?

The Bible never explicitly describes babies being baptized. It does describe entire households being baptized, which may have included young children. However, the Bible never describes the way we should baptize someone, and that doesn't stop us from baptizing people.

Should we pour water over a person's head? Should we fully immerse him in water? Could we just sprinkle water on people, especially if they live in places like the desert, which barely has any water? God's written word doesn't tell us, but God's spoken word, preserved in Sacred Tradition, does. The *Didache* records how the first-century Church practiced baptism:

> Concerning baptism, baptize in this manner: having said all these things beforehand, baptize in the name of the Father and of the Son and of the Holy Spirit in living water [that is, in running water, as in a river]. If there is no living water, baptize in other water; and, if you are not able to use cold water, use warm. If you have neither, pour water three times upon the head in the name of the Father, Son, and Holy Spirit.[33]

The Bible and the early Church also never *prohibit* baptism for young children. In light of that fact, it is safe to assume small children can be baptized. Indeed, Hebrews 8:6 teaches that the New Covenant in Christ is greater than the Old Covenant God had with Israel. Since the Old Covenant included babies through circumcision, this means the New Covenant must also include babies, or else it would be inferior to the Old Covenant. This is why, as we noted earlier, Paul calls baptism "the circumcision of Christ" in Colossians 2:11-12.

Some in the early Church believed that baptism's replacement of circumcision meant parents had to wait eight days to baptize their children, since that's how long people waited to circumcise babies in the Old Covenant. But the Fathers of the Church said babies should be baptized as soon as possible, especially since it was tragically common for children in that time to die soon after birth. In a document commonly attributed to the third-century author Hippolytus, he advised his readers to "baptize the little children first. And if they can answer for themselves, let them answer. But if they cannot, let their parents answer or someone from their family."[34]

During the same time period, Cyprian said, "The mercy and grace of God ought to be denied to no man born. . . . No one is held back from baptism and grace. How much more, then, should an infant not be held back?"[35] The ecclesiastical writer Origen said, "The Church has received the tradition from the apostles to give baptism even to little children. For they to whom the secrets of the divine mysteries were committed were aware that in everyone was [original] sin's innate defilement, which needed to be washed away through water and the Spirit."[36]

Finally, the late Protestant apologist R.C. Sproul defended infant baptism: "The fact that the practice of infant baptism seems to have spread to the whole Christian community within a hundred years with no known protest is a further indication that the acceptability of giving infant children the covenant sign was simply assumed by the early Church."[37]

Are Babies Sinners?

Some Protestants say that infants do not need to be baptized because they have never committed any sins, and so they will go straight to heaven. But no one can earn heaven on his own abilities (even if he has never sinned) because heaven is God's gift to creatures—it can't be earned and isn't deserved. And since it is his gift, he can give it to anyone—even children who die before receiving baptism. But we cannot presume God will always act in extraordinary ways (otherwise they wouldn't be extra-ordinary!), so we must be faithful to the ordinary ways he gave us to save people from sin, like baptizing them.

Presuming that babies go to heaven because they've never committed an actual sin also ignores the doctrine of original sin, the teaching that we inherited an absence of sanctifying grace from Adam and Eve and so we have a fallen human nature that needs to be redeemed.

The reason this absence of grace is called "original sin" is that it is a consequence of the first sin humans committed. When our first parents, Adam and Eve, disobeyed God, they lost the gift of God's favor that protected them from death and suffering. After losing this grace, they could not pass it down to their descendants, who in turn could not pass it down to us. Adam and Eve's disobedience corrupted our human nature and made it possible for humans to suffer and die. It's why, as I noted earlier, Psalm 51:5 says, "Behold, I was brought forth in iniquity, and in sin did my mother conceive me."

Baptism cannot prevent our physical deaths because it does not change our physical nature. It does, however, change our spiritual nature. Through baptism we are saved from spiritual death by being united to Jesus Christ.

Some people say it's not fair for God to punish us because of something Adam and Eve did, but original sin is not a punishment. It is a *consequence* of what Adam and Eve did, which we have to endure, like if your great-grandfather gambled away your family fortune, causing you to be born into poverty.

One man's disobedience cursed humanity, but another man's obedience saved it (Rom. 5:19). Paul says that we are freed from sin by dying and rising with Christ, but how exactly do we do that? Through baptism, as he explains in Romans 6:3-4: "Do you not know that all of us who have been baptized into Christ Jesus were baptized into his death? We were buried therefore with him by baptism into death, so that as Christ was raised from the dead by the glory of the Father, we too might walk in newness of life."

Denying babies God's grace through baptism because we think it is better for them to consciously choose it later as an adult would be like denying a baby medicine so that he can choose "for himself" to take the medicine when he gets older. Original sin is just too serious to leave in anyone's body, especially a child's. God can save anyone who was unable to receive baptism, but that doesn't give us license to ignore this ordinary means of salvation and sanctification. That's why even though I was baptized as an adult, I give all my children shortly after they're born a gift I wasn't blessed with at their age: the grace of God, poured into their hearts through the sacrament of baptism.

But why does it have to be baptism in the *Catholic* Church?

The Catholic Church teaches that nearly all Protestant denominations have valid baptisms because they use the right material (water), the right words ("in the name of the Father, and the Son, and the Holy Spirit"), and the right intention (to do what Jesus commanded [Matt. 28:19]). Other Christian baptisms are valid because God wants to save all people (1 Tim. 2:4), and so he has made this sacrament one that can be widely administered.

The Church teaches that although the ordinary minister of baptism is a priest or a deacon, in an emergency, anyone, even a non-Christian, can validly baptize if he uses the right material (matter) and the right words (form) and has the right intention (to do what the Church does in baptism). The *Catechism* says, "Through baptism we are freed from sin and reborn as sons of God; we become members of Christ, are incorporated into the Church and made sharers in her mission" (1213).

Whereas non-Catholic baptisms partially incorporate a person into Christ's Church, Catholic baptism fully unites him to the Church. This is important because baptism is merely the beginning of our spiritual journey. The *Catechism* says,

"Holy baptism is the basis of the whole Christian life, the gateway to life in the Spirit, and the door which gives access to the other sacraments" (1213).

Through baptism, all our previous sins, as well as the stain of original sin that we inherited from Adam and Eve, are washed away. But what happens if a Christian seriously sins after baptism? Christ gives us the answer: just as it is ordinarily necessary to approach a minister of the Church the first time we are freed from grave sin, it is just as necessary to approach a minister of the Church to be freed from grave sin *after* baptism. It's why Jesus told the apostles, "If you forgive the sins of any, they are forgiven; if you retain the sins of any, they are retained" (John 20:23).

And this brings us to the fifth way salvation is from the Catholic Church: it gives us the sacrament of reconciliation.

CHAPTER 6

Right *Reconciliation*

The Catholic Church saves us through its ministers, who communicate God's forgiveness of sins.

When people ask me why they need to go to see a priest in confession instead of going "directly to God," I remind them that they already believe that you can't "go directly to God" when it comes to another sacrament: baptism.

Protestants believe that someone else (ideally, a Church minister) has to baptize you—you can't baptize yourself. Protestants who believe that baptism saves us from sin consequently believe that we need the involvement of a minister of the Church if we want to obtain the forgiveness of sins that leads to our initial salvation.

But if we need that involvement from a minister of the Church the *first* time we go from being dead in sin to being alive in Christ, then why wouldn't we need the Church's minister the other times we fall from grace and seek to be reconciled to God? Paul even says in 2 Corinthians 5:18, "Christ reconciled us to himself and gave us the ministry of reconciliation." In the fourth century, St. Ambrose, the teacher of St. Augustine, said, "If baptism is certainly the remission of all sins, what difference does it make whether priests claim that this power is given to them in penance [confession] or at the font?"[38]

I'm not saying you will go to hell if you are unable to confess your sins to a priest. As we saw with baptism, God can save people in extraordinary ways if they are unable to seek him through the ordinary ways he gave us. But we should not presume upon extraordinary ways of salvation if we can seek the ordinary ways God gave us, one of which is the confession of sins to a priest of Christ's Church.

"If We Confess Our Sins . . ."

I want to be clear that confession is not a work we do to earn salvation. We can't even approach God on our own when we are in a state of mortal sin and separated from him. In that case, God gives us *actual grace* (a spiritual kick in the pants, if you will) that moves us to seek him in the confessional and to be restored in friendship with him through his grace, which sanctifies our souls.

So, when St. Paul, quoting David, says, "Blessed is the man against whom the Lord will not reckon his sin" (Rom. 4:8), he is referring to anyone who experiences the blessedness of God's forgiveness. This does not mean that after we are saved, God simply looks the other way and doesn't "count" future sins against us. It means that when God forgives us, our sins will no longer be held against us or "reckoned" to us, and God is always waiting as a merciful Father to forgive our faults, no matter how big we tiny humans think they are. Indeed, it is God who forgives sins, not a priest. Paragraph 1441 of the *Catechism* says,

> Only God forgives sins. Since he is the Son of God, Jesus says of himself, "The Son of man has authority on earth to forgive sins" and exercises this divine power: "Your sins are forgiven." Further, by virtue of his divine

> authority he gives this power to men to exercise in his name.

God forgives sins, and he does so through a minister of the Church. Although Jesus taught his disciples to ask God to forgive us our trespasses, the New Testament authors never say that we should confess particular or individual sins to God. Instead, confession and the forgiveness of sins is bound up in the authority of the ministers of the Church.

At this, many Protestants bring up 1 John 1:9: "If we confess our sins, he is faithful and just, and will forgive our sins and cleanse us from all unrighteousness." Doesn't this mean that all we must do is confess our sins to God?

Well, that assumes that the recipient of the verb "confess" in this passage is God. But in John's letter, the recipients of that verb are other human beings. In 1 John 2:23, he says, "No one who denies the Son has the Father. He who confesses the Son has the Father also." This is referring to the confession we make to other people, not to God. 1 John 1:9 is bracketed by verses that also refer to what we say to other people.

> Verse 8: "If *we say* we have no sin, we deceive ourselves, and the truth is not in us."
>
> Verse 9: "If *we confess* our sins, he is faithful and just, and will forgive our sins and cleanse us from all unrighteousness."
>
> Verse 10: "If *we say* we have not sinned, we make him a liar, and his word is not in us."

There's no reason to think verse 9 refers to what we privately say to God and not what we say to other people. The Greek word *homologeo*, which is translated "confess" in this verse, means, "I confess, profess, acknowledge, praise." It is used twenty-six times in the New Testament. Each time it is used, with one exception, it refers to a person publicly declaring something to another human being. It is never used to refer to confessing sins to God. In John's writings, it always used to describe confessing something to another human being.

"If You Forgive the Sins of Any . . ."

The only place where confession of sins is mentioned in Scripture is James 5:16, which says, "Therefore confess your sins to one another, and pray for one another, that you may be healed." In the context James is referring to the elders, the *presbyteroi*, from which we get the English word *priest*, who anoint the sick. James says in verse 15, "The prayer of faith will save the sick man, and the Lord will raise him up; and if he has committed sins, he will be forgiven." Notice this is joined with the conjunction "therefore" (in Greek, *oun*). This places the confession of sins to one another in the context of seeking out the Church's priests.

John's Gospel describes Jesus appearing to the disciples after his resurrection and says, "He breathed on them, and said to them, 'Receive the Holy Spirit. If you forgive the sins of any, they are forgiven; if you retain the sins of any, they are retained'" (20:22-23). Protestants claim that in John 20:23, Jesus was giving the apostles the power only to *preach* the forgiveness of sins—not the ability to communicate the forgiveness of sins through a sacrament. But in John's Gospel, Jesus rarely refers to the preaching of the apostles, and the subject is not mentioned in this chapter. In verse 23, Jesus simply says, "If you forgive the sins of any, they are forgiven."

Others say that the Greek in this verse means that the text should actually say, "If you forgive the sins of any, they have already been forgiven," which implies that they were just preaching the forgiveness of sins and were not ministers of forgiveness on Christ's behalf. But the Greek in this passage doesn't mean that the apostles merely announced the forgiveness of sins.

Consider Jesus' declaration about the sinful woman who anointed his head at the house of Simon the Pharisee. He said, "Her sins, which are many, are forgiven [*aphiami*, the same word in John 20:23], for [or because] she loved much" (Luke 7:47). Notice that the woman's sins were forgiven *after* she demonstrated her love for Jesus. New Testament professor James Barker says the grammar of this passage "conveys that God concurs with the disciples' decision, and the perfect aspect [or tense, for our purposes here] signifies the enduring significance of the disciples' decisions." In the fourth century, St. John Chrysostom understood John 20:23 in the same way: "What priests do here below, God ratifies above."[39]

Chrysostom's understanding of confession can also be seen in many other voices from the early Church.

Medicine for the Soul

The *Catechism* says that even though the disciplines related to the sacrament of confession have changed over time, the sacrament has always maintained a certain fundamental structure (1447-1448). Specifically, the sacrament includes the sinner expressing repentance for his sins and God, working through the ministers of the Church, healing the sinner and re-establishing him in ecclesial communion with the body of Christ.

In the first century, the *Didache* gave believers the following instruction: "In your gatherings, confess your transgressions, and do not come for prayer with a guilty conscience" (4:14). In the second century, St. Irenaeus describes women who were taken in by the heretic Marcius, saying some of them "make a public confession of their sins; but others of them are ashamed to do this, and in a tacit kind of way, despairing of [attaining to] the life of God."[40]

In the third century, St. Cyprian of Carthage gives this advice: "Let each one confess his sin, I beseech you, brethren, while he who has sinned is still in this world, while his confession can be admitted, while the satisfaction and remission effected through the priest is pleasing with the Lord."[41]

God gave us sacraments because we matter, and we are made of matter. The liquid water poured over our bodies in baptism reminds us that this sacrament washes our sins away (Acts 22:16). When Jesus told the apostles, "He who hears you hears me" (Luke 10:16), this applies in a way to God's priests, who give us a similar comfort when Christ speaks the following words through them in the confessional: "I absolve you of your sins."

Christ is also the divine physician, and confessing sins to a priest is like telling a doctor an embarrassing health problem. I understand why such an act would be initially uncomfortable. But isn't it funny that we are embarrassed about what another human being thinks of our sins, and we don't have that sense of embarrassment or shame when we bring our sins to God in prayer?

God gave us this sacrament so that we would more profoundly experience the bad news of our sins and the good news of his forgiveness. It's why Cyprian gave this advice: "Confess this very thing to God's priests, and make the conscientious avowal, put off from them the load of their minds, and seek out the salutary medicine even for slight and moderate wounds."[42]

There is also a sense of deep comfort in being able to approach in the flesh another person who is a channel of God's mercy and tell him sins you wouldn't tell anyone else because you know he's bound to keep them secret. If a priest ever violates the "seal of the confessional," he is automatically excommunicated. He can never, under any circumstance, reveal the sins you've confessed to him. And many priests I know say God gives them a special grace to forget the sins they hear in confession.

Just as baptism marks a definite sign that we have been cleansed of sin, and so we don't have to doubt if we were really saved, sacramental confession marks a definite sign that we have been received back into communion with Christ and his church, and we don't have to worry about if we "did enough" to come back into God's graces. We simply do what we did in our baptism: bring our sins to the minister of God's church and accept God's gift of salvation from them.

CHAPTER 7

Right *Pastors*

The Catholic Church shepherds us with authority.

Acts 11:26 says it was in the city of Antioch that the followers of Jesus were first called Christians. Just a few decades later, in the same city, the followers of Jesus were called *Catholics*. The word *Catholic* comes from the Greek words *kata-holos*, "according to the whole" or "universal." St. Ignatius, the bishop of Antioch, used the word when he wrote the following just a few decades after Christ's crucifixion:

> Wherever the bishop shall appear, there let the multitude [of the people] also be; even as, wherever Jesus Christ is, there is the Catholic Church. It is not lawful without the bishop either to baptize or to celebrate a love-feast [that is, a meal before the Eucharist]; but whatsoever he shall approve of, that is also pleasing to God, so that everything that is done may be secure and valid.[43]

For Ignatius, the "church" was not a loose designation for all Christians who, despite their theological differences, believe in the Bible. In Ignatius's time, *there was no Christian Bible*. There were some writings from the apostles (which Ignatius doesn't call "Scripture"), but they weren't treated as the Church's ultimate authority. In fact, the Apostles' Creed, one of the oldest creeds in Church history, *never mentions Scripture*.

Instead, it says that belief in "the holy catholic Church" is a necessary part of the Faith.

Can Jesus Be Your Pastor?

By the end of the second century, over 150 years after Christ's resurrection, people like Irenaeus, a bishop in southern France, began to refer to the "New Testament." But Irenaeus did not believe in *sola scriptura*. He even asks, "How should it be if the apostles themselves had not left us writings? Would it not be necessary to follow the course of the tradition which they handed down?"[44]

Irenaeus viewed the successors of the apostles as the guardians of this tradition, which is why he gives us the earliest list of all the successors of the bishop of Rome, whom Catholics call the *pope*. The fourth member of that list, Clement, wrote during the time of the apostles and gives us this key insight into the early Church's structure of leadership:

> Our apostles knew, through our Lord Jesus Christ, that there would be strife on account of the office of the episcopate. For this reason, therefore, inasmuch as they had obtained a perfect foreknowledge of this, they appointed those [ministers] already mentioned, and afterward gave instructions, that when these should fall asleep, other approved men should succeed them in their ministry.[45]

Most Christians recognize the importance of having a good pastor overseeing your spiritual life. I remember one Protestant apologist recounting a story of talking with two obnoxious young men who belonged to his theological tradition. After seeing their conversation became unproductive, he decided to speak to their pastor about their behavior. He asked them, "Who is your elder?," to which they responded, "Jesus is our elder!"

He reminded them that Hebrews 13:17 says, "Obey your leaders and submit to them; for they are keeping watch over your souls, as men who will have to give account." He expected them as Christians to be in submission to a pastor, who would give them spiritual guidance and reprove their misbehavior.

But by what authority can another man be a spiritual authority over me? Is it because he went to seminary? Is it because a bunch of people already like his church?

The Bible *never* describes a Christian starting his own church—a pastor always had to be ordained by someone with apostolic authority, such as how Acts 14:23 describes how the apostles "appointed elders for them in every church." The Protestant scholar Craig Keener says, "The earliest Jewish Christians would have been familiar with laying on of hands for ordination before it was practiced among themselves (1 Tim. 4:14)."[46]

In the Old Testament, God's people had a three-tiered priesthood that has been fulfilled in Christ's Church. First, the people as a whole were called a kingdom of priests, because their holy conduct would allow them to intercede on behalf of an unbelieving world (Exod. 19:6). Some of them, like the Levites, were part of the ministerial priesthood and offered sacrifices on behalf of the people (28:41). Finally, there was the high priest, who approached God's sacred dwelling among the people once a year to offer a sacrifice that made up for the people's sins as a whole (28:1, Lev. 21:10).

Just like in the Old Testament, St. Peter says every Christian belongs to a holy priesthood (1 Pet. 2:5). The letter to the Hebrews says Jesus Christ is our new high priest (4:14) and that the priests who offer Christ on the altar become the fulfillment of the ministerial priesthood of the Old Testament. This makes sense because the power to make bread and wine become the body and blood of Jesus Christ can't belong to just anyone who utters a special prayer. To offer the Eucharist is to offer sacrifice to God—something only priests can do. And nobody can become a priest by declaring himself a priest, just as no one can become a Christian by just declaring himself one.

In order to become Christian, a person must be baptized by someone else. But as we've seen, because God wants all to be saved, anyone (even an atheist) can do this. However, God does not intend for all people to become priests who offer the Eucharist. The only way to become a priest—i.e., to receive the sacrament of holy orders—is to receive it from someone who has that sacrament—namely, a bishop. That's why in the New Testament, the only way to receive a spiritual office in the Church was when the hands of an apostle or his associate were laid upon you.

This is why Ignatius told his listeners, "See that you all follow the bishop, even as Jesus Christ does the Father, and the presbytery as you would the apostles."[47] In another letter, he says, "Let all reverence the deacons as an appointment of Jesus Christ, and the bishop as Jesus Christ, who is the Son of the Father, and the presbyters as the Sanhedrin of God, and assembly of the apostles. Apart from these, there is no Church.[48]

The One Foundation of Truth

How many churches did Christ establish? One. Christ established one church, which he called "my church." That's why Ephesians 4:5 says we have "one Lord, one faith, one baptism" and in the Nicene Creed we say we believe "in *one*, holy, catholic, and apostolic Church" and we "confess *one* baptism for the forgiveness of sins."

Some Protestants say this one church does exist, but it is invisible. "The church" is just a way to refer to all Christians, and every local church is one expression of this larger, universal invisible church.

Except that can't possibly be true.

In his letter to Timothy, Paul exhorts his disciple to know how to behave in the Church of the living God, which he calls "the pillar and foundation of the truth" (1 Tim. 3:15). The Church helps us understand the truth God has revealed, but how can "the collection of Christians" do that when they can't agree on what God said about baptism, the Eucharist, whether salvation can be lost, who should lead the Church . . . and, ironically enough, who even counts as a Christian who belongs to said Church?

Many Protestants say a new Christian should pick a church that most closely aligns with his view of what the Bible teaches. But how can "the Church" lead me to the truth of what Christ teaches if one of the ways I pick a church is based on whether *I* think it preaches that truth in the first place?

Under this view, "the church" doesn't lead me to true doctrine. Instead, my understanding of doctrine leads me to a local church, and then it is my job to lead whatever church I joined to what *I* think is true doctrine. If a necessary condition of the one Church Christ founded is that it can lead me to truths God has revealed, then this proves that the "universal, invisible church" is not Christ's Church, because its cacophony of disagreeing denominations can't lead me to that truth.

Christ also said, "The gates of hell will not prevail against" the Church (Matt. 16:18), and so that means this one, visible authoritative church must still exist somewhere on the face of the earth. Indeed, Christ promised that it would exist because he gave it the power to discipline believers. Jesus told his listeners in Matthew 18:17 that if a brother sins against them that, as a matter of last resort, the brother should be brought "to the Church" for a judgment. The Protestant author D.A. Carson observes that "only 'church' (*ekklesia* in the singular) is used for the congregation of all believers in one city, never 'churches.'"[49]

But how can "the church" discipline me if I am always free to join a different denomination?

Sure, a local Christian body could say I'm no longer welcome to attend their church, but they can't separate me from "the church," because the church is just all Christians. Even if an entire Protestant denomination denounced someone, that denomination can't speak for "the church," because within Protestantism no one can speak for "the church." One denomination might excommunicate a person for defending "gay marriage," but another denomination might consider him a heroic part of "the church." This has happened in the past few years with Episcopalians and Methodists, who split into separate sub-groups over this very issue.

The Bible is clear that sometimes a person must be removed from Christ's Church, and not just a single denomination. This is done both for his good and for the good of the other members of Christ's body. St. Paul demanded that a member of the Corinthian congregation who engaged in incest with his stepmother be "handed over to Satan." He had to be taken out of communion (ex-communicated) from the Church so "that his spirit may be saved in the day of the Lord Jesus" (1 Cor. 5:5).

Part of this punishment involved being prohibited from receiving the Eucharist because, as we previously noted, receiving the Eucharist while in grave sin causes the receiver to eat and drink judgment on himself (1 Cor. 11:29), and the Church doesn't want sinners to compound their sins by receiving communion with Christ when they are not truly in communion with him and his church.

The Sin of Schism

If Christ established one church that has visible authority over believers, then where do that church and its authority exist today? And if that church still exists, don't we have an obligation to formally belong to *that* church instead of trying to form our own churches? In his first letter to the Corinthians, Paul warned about divisions in the Church, saying, "I appeal to you, brethren, by the name of our Lord Jesus Christ, that all of you agree and that there be no dissensions among you, but that you be united in the same mind and the same judgment" (1:10).

The word "dissension" is similar in meaning to the Greek word *schismata*, from which we also get the word *schism*. Schism is the sin of rejecting the authority of Christ's Church that is found among the successors of the apostles. Paul himself warned about Christians who rejected this authority and claimed to belong instead to their favorite pastor. He even rebukes those who said, "I belong to Christ"—the first-century equivalent of saying, "Jesus is my elder!" St. Ignatius gives a more direct prohibition in his letter to the Philadelphians:

> For as many as are of God and of Jesus Christ are also with the bishop. And as many as shall, in the exercise of repentance, return into the unity of the Church, these, too, shall belong to God, that they may live according to Jesus Christ.

> Do not err, my brethren. If any man follows him that makes a schism in the Church, he shall not inherit the kingdom of God. If any one walks according to a strange opinion, he agrees not with the Passion [of Christ].
>
> Take heed, then, to have but one Eucharist. For there is one flesh of our Lord Jesus Christ, and one cup to [show] the unity of his blood; one altar; as there is one bishop, along with the presbytery and deacons, my fellow-servants: that so, whatsoever you do, you may do it according to [the will of] God."[50]

The Protestant Reformers also believed that schism was sinful and that the Church (however they might define that) has authority over believers. John Calvin imposed a set of ecclesiastical ordinances on the city of Geneva along with a special court to enforce them. They said, "Certain crimes are quite incompatible with the ministry and cannot be dealt with by fraternal rebuke. Namely heresy, schism, rebellion against Church discipline." Church attendance was mandatory, and "leaving the Church without special permission" was a punishable offense.[51]

Some scholars estimate that one in fifteen people in Geneva was brought before the Calvinist church's court, and one in twenty-five was excommunicated.[52] One of the most common charges was "contradicting the ministers," as lay people were not free to interpret doctrine for themselves. One citizen named Pierre Amareux was readmitted to the Church only after he crawled on his hands and knees to the bishop's house. He probably feared for his immortal soul, since Calvin said excommunication meant one was "estranged from the Church, and thus, from Christ."[53]

Even the Reformers believed that the faithful must submit to human pastors, lest they risk their immortal souls.

This stands in continuity with the early Church Fathers, who taught that the Church is the "ark" of our salvation. Just as Noah and his family were saved from the Flood by residing within the ark, sinners are saved from sin by residing within the Church. Cyprian said in the third century, "He who was not in the ark of Noah could not be saved by water, so neither can he appear to be saved by baptism who has not been baptized in the Church which is established in the unity of the Lord according to the sacrament of the one ark."[54]

From the beginning, Christians understood that to be saved, one must remain in union not just with Christ, but with the visible Church he created to guide believers to salvation. One of the reasons is that it was to this Church that Christ entrusted the priesthood and the administering of sacraments like the Eucharist that give us eternal life. The Church also acts as a surrogate parent, who guides our growth and educates us in the truths God has revealed, rather than leaving those truths as something to be discovered in individual study of Scripture.

And the figure that binds our spiritual fathers together is the successor of the apostolic Church's spiritual father: St. Peter.

CHAPTER 8

Right *"Senior Pastor"*

The Catholic Church keeps us in union with the divinely instituted overseer of Christ's Church.

Once, in a debate where I joined Jimmy Akin against two Protestants, one of the audience members asked, "If the Roman Catholic Church says it's absolutely necessary for salvation that 'every creature submit to the Roman pontiff,' what happens to the justification of a Christian who willingly refuses to submit the Catholic Church?"

The questioner was quoting a papal bull called *Unam Sanctam*, which says that to be saved, one must submit to the authority of the pope. Jimmy began the response by noting that God won't damn a person who is ignorant of his duty to become Catholic, just as he won't damn someone who is merely ignorant of his duty to become Christian. However, if someone knows that Jesus is God or that the Catholic Church is the Church Christ established, refusal to submit to either could lead to damnation.

Our opponent actually agreed with that sentiment and said he had a hard time seeing how someone who removed himself from the Church could still be saved, such as my friend Kevin, whom we met in chapter four, who said he doesn't attend church. Our opponent then said a Christian must obey the bishop, though he qualified his response saying he wasn't able to speak for all Protestants. I reassured him, "Don't worry, nobody can."

St. Cyprian said that one cannot call God "Father" unless he also calls the Church "mother." But Cyprian also noted that God gave a means for the Church to have unity that is needed to provide maternal spiritual guidance. He said, "A primacy is given to Peter, whereby it is made clear that there is but one Church and one chair. . . . If he deserts the chair of Peter upon whom the Church was built, can he still be confident that he is in the Church?"[55]

As we will see, Christ established one Church built upon the apostles, and one of the apostles, Peter, was selected to be the chief apostle, the leader of the Church. If we are to submit to our elders in the Church, then to whom must the elders submit if not the one pastor who is given authority over Christ's Church, whom Catholics call "the pope"?

A True Kingdom of God

Some Protestants are wary of the pope because they see him as a pastor who is celebrated with pomp and circumstance that is foreign to the New Testament. But *pope* is just another word for "father," and St. Paul says he is a spiritual father to the Corinthians (1 Cor. 4:15). The pope is a spiritual father and pastor who oversees all of Christ's Church, including all the successors of the apostles. The first pope was Peter, and although he didn't drive around in a pope-mobile, people did long for his shadow to fall upon them so that they would be healed (Acts 5:15–16).

If people did that to modern popes, I'm sure Protestants would consider that the rankest form of superstition, but St. Luke, the author of Acts, certainly didn't view it that way.

Peter's authority in the Church can be seen from the fact that in the complete lists of the apostles, Peter is always listed first and Judas Iscariot is always listed last—that is, they are listed from "highest" to "lowest." In Matthew 16:18-19, Jesus changed Simon's name to Peter, which means "rock," and said, "You are Peter [rock], and on this rock I will build my church, and the powers of death shall not prevail against it."

In my other books, I answer objections that something besides Peter is "the rock," but one question is enough to put that objection on its heels: Why would Jesus bother changing Simon's name to "rock" if he had nothing to do with "the rock" upon which the Church would be built?

Jesus went on to say, "I will give you the keys of the kingdom of heaven, and whatever you bind on earth shall be bound in heaven, and whatever you loose on earth shall be loosed in heaven." This is an allusion to Isaiah 22:22, which tells of how Israel's wicked chief steward, Shebna, was replaced with the righteous Eliakim. Isaiah 22:22 says Eliakim would have "the key of the house of David; he shall open, and none shall shut; and he shall shut, and none shall open." Just as King Hezekiah gave Eliakim authority to oversee the kingdom of Israel, Christ gave Peter authority (the "keys to the kingdom") to oversee his church, which included the authority to "bind and loose"—in other words, to determine official doctrine and practice.

If you think the Church is just a spiritual collection of believers, then you miss Christ's purpose in inaugurating a kingdom, the kingdom of God, here on earth. This would not be a materialistic kingdom, but it wouldn't be purely spiritual, either. Christ even said the apostles would sit on thrones and judge people (Matt. 19:28). Christ's Church would be a royal kingdom—he is the kingdom, and Peter was to be the prime minister or "chief steward." Protestant church historian J.N.D. Kelly acknowledges that "Peter was the undisputed leader of the youthful church."[56]

In the second century, long before Emperor Constantine allegedly invented the papacy in the fourth century, as some critics allege, Pope St. Victor I excommunicated an entire region of churches for refusing to celebrate Easter on its proper date. Although St. Irenaeus thought this was not prudent, neither he nor anyone else denied that Victor had the authority to do this. Indeed, Irenaeus said, "it is a matter of necessity that every church should agree with this church [Rome] on account of its pre-eminent authority."[57]

When Does the Pope Teach?

It would take a full-length treatment to properly explain the evidence for the divine origins of the papacy, though I have addressed several objections to it in my book *The Case for Catholicism*. Other full-length cases can be found in Joe Heschmeyer's book *Pope Peter* and Erick Ybarra's book *The Papacy*.

My goal here is to show that

1) rejecting the authority of our spiritual elders and refusing to belong to Christ's Church can result in forsaking our salvation,

2) our current spiritual elders are only those men who have received authority from the successors of the apostles, and

3) these pastors have different levels of authority and oblige the faithful to different levels of obedience.

This third point is something many Protestants accept. A Protestant would recognize the authority of his local pastor, but if that pastor strays from the faith, theologically or morally, he has to answer to some other authority. If every pastor were an authority unto himself, then Christ's Church would be not a mystical body, but a chaotic aggregate of different local congregations. Often, the Protestant must answer to a group of elders or, among some Protestants like Anglicans, a bishop who oversees all the priests of a particular jurisdiction. The Eastern Orthodox have also maintained the role of the bishop or patriarch in providing authority over priests as guardians of the Faith.

But *quis custodiet ipsos custodes*? In English: who will guard the guardians?

Just as a king unifies the lords who rule a kingdom, a prime minister unifies the politicians of a state, and a CEO unifies the managers of a company, the successor of St. Peter unifies the Church, just as Peter himself did. Jesus even entrusted Peter with the task of strengthening his brethren, knowing full well that he would fail in his role as a leader by denying Christ. He told him, "Satan has demanded to sift you all like wheat, but I have prayed for you that your faith may not fail; and when you have turned again, strengthen your brethren" (Luke 22:31-32). The original Greek in the passage shows that Satan demanded to sift "you all," or all the apostles, but Jesus prayed only for Peter (since he used the singular "you") for Peter's faith not to fail.

Belonging to Christ's Church means belonging under the authority of the successors of Christ's apostles, the bishops united to St. Peter's successor—the bishop of Rome, or the pope.

Does that mean that Christians have to do everything the pope says? No, because not everything the pope says is meant to be a teaching for the Church, just as not everything the Bible says (like certain ritual laws of the Old Testament) is a rule Christians must follow today. But whereas the Bible is free from error in everything it asserts, the same is not true of the pope.

At the lowest level of authority, the pope leads the Church through exhortations and prudential judgments. The faithful give deference to these, but not religious submission of their minds and wills. However, when the pope formally teaches as the pastor of the entire Church, the faithful must obey those teachings, which ensures that the Church has a living voice with Christ's authority to guide believers to salvation. We've already seen how a pope did this in modern times by opposing gestational surrogacy in the twenty-first century and abortion and contraception in the twentieth. Pope John Paul II gave a highly authoritative teaching on abortion in his encyclical *Evangelium Vitae* that echoed what Pope Pius XI said in 1930, when legalized abortion began to rear its head:

> By the authority which Christ conferred upon Peter and his successors, in communion with the bishops . . . I declare that direct abortion, that is, abortion willed as an end or as a means, always constitutes a grave moral disorder, since it is the deliberate killing of an innocent human being. This doctrine is based upon the natural law and upon the written word of God, is transmitted by the Church's Tradition and taught by the ordinary and universal Magisterium (62).

John Paul II reaffirmed that the Church has infallibly taught that abortion is immoral through its constant and universal teaching across space and time for 2,000 years. And unlike Protestant ministers or even the Eastern Orthodox patriarchs, the pope was able to speak to the entire Church in a universal way that commands the assent of the faithful.

Doctrines like this one have been reaffirmed so prominently and unceasingly in Church history that they do not have to be specially defined at an ecumenical council like other doctrines that were declared in the face of some heresy (like a denial of Christ's divinity). But there is a third category of infallible teaching beyond the ordinary and universal Magisterium and the solemn declarations of ecumenical councils.

On a minority of occasions, the pope can teach infallibly as the pastor overseeing the entire Church in Christ's stead. The doctrine of papal infallibility teaches that the pope has a special grace from God that protects him from leading the Church into error. That grace won't give him the right answer to every problem facing the Church. But it will protect the pope from solemnly binding the Church to the wrong answer, or some kind of error in faith or morals. As a private theologian, the pope might speculate, even incorrectly, about the Faith. However, he will never issue a false teaching related to faith or morality that claims to bind the entire Church to an infallible judgment. These kinds of infallible papal teachings are called *ex cathedra*, because they are issued from the chair or authority of St. Peter himself.

Papal infallibility doesn't mean the pope will also be courageous and virtuous. Some popes engaged in serious sins, such as fornication, but infallibility means only that the pope won't teach error, not that he will be sinless (that's called *impeccability*). Some Church Fathers, such as St. Cyprian of Carthage, criticized the pope's decisions, but even Cyprian believed that the pope could not lead the Church astray. He wrote in the middle of the third century about heretics who come "to the throne of Peter, and to the chief church whence priestly unity takes its source; and not to consider that these were the Romans whose faith was praised in the preaching of the apostle, to whom faithlessness could have no access"—or, as other translations put it, "from whom no error can flow."[58]

Where Peter Is

Protestant communities often split over hot-button moral issues, especially homosexuality, leaving Christians with the unenviable task of choosing where to go by weighing the arguments of each seceding denomination to see "where the truth went." But when schism occurred in the Church in the past, the answer of whom to follow was not whoever could win a doctrinal debate. It was found in who could prove his connection to the apostles.

This is why the Church Fathers said, "Where Peter is, there is the Church," which means that rejecting Peter (or his successors) risks rejecting Christ's Church, the ark of our salvation. St. Augustine criticized the Donatist heretics, saying their counterfeit bishops did not have a historical connection to the apostles as the Catholic bishops had. He wrote,

> If the lineal succession of bishops is to be taken into account, with how much more certainty and benefit to the Church do we reckon back till we reach Peter himself, to whom, as bearing in a figure the whole Church, the Lord said, "Upon this rock will I build my Church, and the gates of hell shall not prevail against it"! The successor of Peter was Linus, and his successors in unbroken continuity were these . . .

Augustine then lists the thirty-seven bishops of Rome in Church history up to his time before saying, "In this order of succession no Donatist bishop is found."[59] St. Ambrose, Augustine's teacher, decried the heretical Novatianists, saying,

> They have not the succession of Peter, who hold not the chair of Peter, which they rend by wicked schism; and this, too, they do, wickedly denying that sins can

> be forgiven even in the Church, whereas it was said to Peter, "I will give unto thee the keys of the kingdom of heaven, and whatsoever thou shalt bind on earth shall be bound also in heaven, and whatsoever thou shalt loose on earth shall be loosed also in heaven."[60]

Finally, St. Jerome asked Pope Damasus to resolve the issue of the rightful claimant to the See of Antioch, saying, "As I follow no leader save Christ, so I communicate with none but your blessedness, that is with the chair of Peter. For this, I know, is the rock on which the church is built!"[61]

As early as the third and fourth centuries, the Church Fathers compared the Church to a ship, with the bishop being the captain. St. Peter referred to how we are saved in baptism like how the occupants of Noah's ark were saved (1 Pet. 3:20-21). Catholics follow the successor of Peter for the same reason Catholics have followed him for the past 2,000 years: he steers the barque of Peter, the Church, and is entrusted with divine protection to guide souls to salvation.

CHAPTER 9

Right *Spiritual Reinforcements*

The Catholic Church equips us with spiritual armaments to protect us in our spiritual combat.

It seemed like just another rowdy pool party until Martha walked out on to the pool deck and saw her worst nightmare: her six-year-old son lying face down at the bottom of the pool.

Martha's husband dove into the water, pulled their son to the surface, and immediately began performing CPR. Within minutes, an ambulance had left the house, speeding their still unresponsive son to the nearest hospital. The sirens faded into the background, replaced with the sounds of shallow hyperventilating, sobs, and hushed prayers among the largely Protestant group of friends who had been with them at the party.

Several attendees began a "prayer chain" via text message and email, imploring everyone they knew to "storm the gates of heaven" with their prayers for this little boy. A few hours later, the boy woke up at the hospital, and the prayers seemed to have been answered: he was going to be all right and could go home later that day.

I tell this story because it reveals something about how God saves us that is often missing from Protestant contexts until a crisis brings it to the surface.

I've known many Protestants who consider devotion to Mary and the saints a distraction at best and idolatry at worst. Why do Catholics pray to them when they can just go directly to Jesus for their needs? Well, why did the attendees at this pool party feel the need to "invade heaven" with prayers from as many different people as possible? Why didn't this boy's parents just rest secure, knowing they could go directly to Jesus with their urgent request to save their son's life?

They didn't, because they know that believers all belong to the body of Christ. Our union with Christ allows our spirit-led requests to truly bless other people and even save them from evil. St. Paul says in 1 Corinthians 12:12, "The body is one and has many members, and all the members of the body, though many, are one body, so it is with Christ." He reaffirms in his letter to the Romans that "we, though many, are one body in Christ, and individually members one of another" (12:5). In addition, God desires that "there may be no discord in the body, but that the members may have the same care for one another. If one member suffers, all suffer together; if one member is honored, all rejoice together" (1 Cor. 12:25-26).

This helps us see that Catholic veneration of Mary and the saints is not, as some Protestants allege, idolatry or even just a distraction that leads us away from Christ. It is one of the ways that God saves us—not just from the evils of this life, but from the ultimate evil of permanently forsaking God and his gift of salvation.

The Communion of Saints

Some people say there's no point in asking Mary or the saints in heaven to pray for us because they are "dead." But death does not divide the body of Christ, because Christ has defeated death. In Revelation 1:18, Jesus says he holds the keys to death, and Jesus in John's Gospel says he is the vine and we are the branches (15:5). If that's true, then how could death ever completely separate the branches from one another as long as they are all spiritually connected to the same vine?

Jesus also said in Mark 12 that God "is not the God of the dead, but of the living" (v. 27) and reminded the Jewish leaders that the Father said, "I am [not 'I was'] the God of Abraham, and the God of Isaac, and the God of Jacob" (v. 26). To write off the saints in heaven as being dead ignores the fact that, because of their union with Christ, they are more alive in heaven than they were on earth.

Hebrews 12:1 provides an explicit reference to the saints in heaven having knowledge of what happens on earth. Throughout Hebrews 11, the author praises Old Testament heroes of the faith like Abraham, Moses, and David. Then, in the first verse of chapter 12 (which in the original work was not separated into chapters), the author says, "Therefore, since we are surrounded by so great a cloud of witnesses, let us also lay aside every weight, and sin which clings so closely, and let us run with perseverance the race that is set before us." The Protestant scholar William Barclay says of this passage, "Christians are like runners in some crowded stadium. As they press on, the crowd looks down; and the crowd looking down are those who have already won the crown."[62]

We also have to recognize that there is a demonic "counter-stadium" in the pits of hell, where the devil and demons cheer for us to fail—to give up on the race and to walk out of the heavenly stadium and into their diabolical abode. In part two of this book, we will see that the Bible teaches that it is possible for a believer to forsake his salvation. Moreover, it's not surprising if he chooses to do that, because there are powerful spiritual forces tempting us to reject God.

That's why Paul gave this instruction to the Ephesians: "Put on the whole armor of God, that you may be able to stand against the wiles of the devil. For we are not contending against flesh and blood, but against the principalities, against the powers, against the world rulers of this present darkness, against the spiritual hosts of wickedness in the heavenly places" (Eph. 6:11-12). And Peter says, "Be sober, be watchful. Your adversary the devil prowls around like a roaring lion, seeking some one to devour. Resist him, firm in your faith, knowing that the same experience of suffering is required of your brotherhood throughout the world" (1 Pet. 5:8-9).

The saints who cheer us on in the cosmic stadium of heaven know what it's like to resist this suffering, and they fervently ask God to help us in this spiritual battle. That's why Paul told the Ephesians, "Keep alert with all perseverance, making supplication for all the saints, and also for me" (Eph. 6:18). This is why I pray for my children's faith every day—and if I were to die tomorrow, I would still be praying for them. Indeed, Revelation 5:8 describes twenty-four elders in heaven who stand before Christ, holding "golden bowls full of incense, which are the prayers of the saints." The *Catechism* says,

> At the present time some of [Christ's] disciples are pilgrims on earth. Others have died and are being purified, while still others are in glory, contemplating "in full light, God himself triune and one, exactly as he is." . . .
>
> The union of the wayfarers with the brethren who sleep in the peace of Christ is in no way interrupted, but on the contrary, according to the constant faith of the Church, this union is reinforced by an exchange of spiritual goods (954-955).

The Bible teaches that the prayers of holy people are more effective than the prayers of less holy people. For example, after Job's friends sinned, Job 42:8–9 records how God instructed them to have Job pray for them. That's because Job was a very good man, and God would hear his prayers. James 5:16 says, "The prayer of a righteous man has great power in its effects"—and who could be more righteous than the saints in heaven, who have been cleansed of all sin, to whom Hebrews 12:23 refers as "the spirits of just men made perfect"? And made not just perfect, but capable of interceding for us before the throne of God.

Now, some Protestants ask me how Mary can hear so many prayers made all at once in different languages. To them I say, "Well, if the devil, a mere creature and an enemy of God, has the ability to tempt billions of people at the same time, why wouldn't God give his friends, the saints, the ability to help billions of members of his spiritual body?"

But is this necessary for salvation? In a strict sense, no.

All that's necessary to be saved is to repent of sin, receive Christ in baptism, and remain united to Christ. You can remain spiritually alive without seeking the intercession of the saints. But you can also remain physically alive without seeking the help of any other human being. There have been many cases throughout history of "feral children," who grew up in the wilderness apart from all human contact. They were physically alive, but their humanity was deeply scarred and at some points almost unrecognizable. That's why the poet John Donne said, "No man is an island"—humans were made to be in communion with one another. This strengthens us to survive not just the physical challenges of life, but the spiritual challenges.

God will not be defeated by any evil creature, but God allows the creatures who love him to carry one another's burdens (Gal. 6:2) and to strengthen one another (Luke 22:32). Paul even references how a spouse can save the person he or she is married to (1 Cor. 7:16). This doesn't mean the person atones for sin, but he leads the other person into deeper union with Christ. Even Protestant parents understand this when they fervently ask God to bring a wayward child back to the Faith. They don't think their recitations mechanically "saved anyone," but they also don't think their requests are merely performative and that God only humors us when he carries out his will. Instead, God's will is always done, but he incorporates us into it, even saying we are his "co-workers" (1 Cor. 3:9).

And like the saints or "holy ones" on earth who eagerly pray for the salvation of all people (1 Tim. 2:4), the saints in heaven always seek to lead people to Jesus Christ. If we would want Christians being sanctified with us in this life to pray for our faith not to falter, then why wouldn't we want Christians who have achieved the blessed goal of complete sanctification to offer the same salvific benefit to us?

A Spiritual Kick in the Pants

As I'll describe in detail in part two, Catholics do not believe they are saved by an arbitrary combination of "faith and works." We instead believe that we are saved by grace, and after that point, we will reach our final salvation in heaven if we do not permanently reject God's offer of salvation here on earth. The only "work" a Catholic must do to be saved is avoiding the evil work of forsaking God and his grace.

Catholics are not "saved by works" in the sense that they must say a certain number of rosaries to get to heaven. You don't have to pray even a single rosary to be saved. These good works save us only in the sense that they spiritually strengthen us. Just as most people don't commit adultery on a whim, most people do not reject God's offer of salvation on a whim. Instead, they gradually allow their souls to be spiritually weakened through freely chosen sins, usually smaller sins. They also neglect to pray and do other works of Christian charity that spiritually revitalize us and draw us into deeper union with God. This leaves them in a spiritually flabby state that makes them more likely to give in to the devil's temptation to commit a grave sin that severs our relationship with God.

St. Paul uses an athletic analogy to show that Christians have to spiritually train for the fight against evil, lest they pay the ultimate price. He says, "Every athlete exercises self-control in all things. They do it to receive a perishable wreath, but we an imperishable. Well, I do not run aimlessly, I do not box as one beating the air; but I pommel my body and subdue it, lest after preaching to others I myself should be disqualified" (1 Cor. 9:25-27).

If even an apostle who experienced a personal revelation and call from Jesus Christ worried that he could forsake his salvation, then we should not be so presumptuous as to think we would never do something so foolish. Instead, the Catholic Church provides a means of salvation through a myriad of spiritual goods that strengthen believers and their walk with Christ.

Among these are the sacraments, or outward signs that communicate an inward reception of God's sanctifying grace that makes a person fit to spend eternity with God. We've already seen how baptism, the Eucharist, and confession of sins to a priest are ways God saves us from sin.

These sacraments should not be confused with *sacramentals*, another form of spiritual goods. The *Catechism* says of these,

> These are sacred signs which bear a resemblance to the sacraments. They signify effects, particularly of a spiritual

> nature, which are obtained through the intercession of the Church. By them men are disposed to receive the chief effect of the sacraments, and various occasions in life are rendered holy (1667).

Sacramentals include sprinkling with holy water and wearing a scapular, though the most common sacramental is the sign of the cross, which Catholics do before they pray. This tradition goes all the way back to the third century, where the ecclesiastical writer Tertullian said, "In all our travels and movements, in all our coming in and going out, in putting on our shoes, at the bath, at the table, in lighting our candles, in lying down, in sitting down, whatever employment occupies us, we mark our forehead with the sign of the cross."[63] In the fourth century, St. Athanasius said, "let him use the sign of that cross which is laughed at among them, and he shall see how by its means demons fly, oracles cease, all magic and witchcraft is brought to nought."[64]

Some Protestants might accuse Catholics of using these things in superstitious ways—and in some cases, they might be right. But there are Protestant analogues to sacramentals. For example, a person might wear a cross necklace, not as a magical amulet, but as a continual reminder of Christ's sacrifice. Or he might tattoo his favorite Bible verse into his skin to keep a reminder of the word of God close to him.

Sacramentals are not strictly necessary for salvation, but Protestants would agree that daily prayer isn't strictly necessary for salvation, either. A person could still be saved even if he spoke to God only once a week. But such behavior would probably risk a person slowly losing his faith or, according to some Protestants, reveal that he "never had a true faith to begin with."

Once again, the spiritual battle is real. St. James tells us that the devil is a threat that we do not fight alone, nor one that we rely on God alone to dispel from our lives. Instead, he says, "Submit yourselves therefore to God. Resist the devil and he will flee from you. Draw near to God and he will draw near to you. Cleanse your hands, you sinners, and purify your hearts, you men of double mind" (James 4:7–8).

This is why the Church provides not just sacramentals, but sacraments, ways of receiving the grace of God, by which we choose pure love of God over disordered love for creatures. And as we will see, the Church's capacity to instill supernatural love for God in our souls is demonstrated in the Church's capacity to recognize God's supernatural intervention—not just in Scripture, but in the past 2,000 years of Church history.

CHAPTER 10

Right *Proofs and Signs*

The Catholic Church miraculously confirms its own divine authority.

Once, when I was sharing the gospel on a college campus to a crowd of students, an atheist in the group challenged me with a barrage of alleged contradictions and atrocities from the Old Testament. This is a common (and underhanded) debating trick, where a person overwhelms his opponent with so many objections that the latter doesn't have time to respond to all of them, and any that are overlooked are declared proof of victory.

The tactic is effective because it can take mere seconds to offer an objection to Christianity ("the Bible endorses slavery") but much longer to rebut one. So, to parry this debating trick, I reframed the issue to keep the conversation on the most important question at hand:

> You're right that there are parts of the Old Testament that are hard to understand and are scandalous to modern ears. When I have more time, I'd be happy to explain all of them to you. But you know what? Jesus Christ believed in the divine authority of the Old Testament, and if a man can walk out of his own tomb, then I'm going to trust what he has to say.

Now, instead of debating peripheral issues about Scripture, we were back to debating the one question that matters most in life, the same question Jesus asked his disciples in Matthew 16:15: "Who do you say that I am?" If Jesus is God, the great "I am," then we should trust his teachings, even if they aren't easy to understand at first. And one way we know that Jesus has divine authority is because he performed a divine act: he miraculously suspended the laws of nature to rise from the dead.

We've now come to the last reason I will offer to believe that salvation comes from the Catholic Church. If we can trust Jesus' message of salvation because it has been vindicated with miracles, then why can't we trust the Catholic Church's message of salvation that has been vindicated with miracles over the past 2,000 years?

The Argument from Miracles

Atheists often try to explain away Christ's resurrection from the dead as a case of grief-induced hallucinations. These do happen to people, but they usually involve only a vague feeling of someone's presence, and they almost always happen to family members of the deceased, not friends (as would be the case with Jesus' disciples). But one of the biggest problems with the hallucination theory is that the historical evidence shows groups of people claiming to have seen Jesus after his death, not single individuals. These include the twelve apostles and even up to 500 others, as recorded in 1 Corinthians 15.

Hallucinations are like dreams: you can't share them, because they are internal and subjective. The best explanation for groups of people claiming to have interacted with the risen Jesus at the same time is that all of those persons really saw the risen Jesus, and this convinced them that he rose from the dead.

In response, atheists claim that group hallucinations can occur. One example they like to share with Protestant defenders of Christ's resurrection is apparitions of the Virgin Mary. Biblical scholar Hector Avalos says Marian apparitions "form the closest parallel to the Jesus apparition stories. . . . Marian apparitions have been reportedly witnessed simultaneously by millions of people, but most evangelical apologists do not see that as proof that Mary is alive."[65] Bart Ehrman likewise notes, "Protestant apologists interested in 'proving' that Jesus was raised from the dead rarely show any interest in applying their finely honed historical talents to the exalted Blessed Virgin Mary."

The argument is compelling because, in some respects, the evidence for groups of people seeing Mary after her death is greater than the evidence that the disciples saw Jesus after his death. For example, skeptics often doubt if the Gospel narratives describing Jesus appearing to the disciples are later legends, but skeptics cannot doubt that groups of people claim to have seen Mary or other miraculous signs.

In 1917, three children in Fatima, Portugal, claimed to have seen the Virgin Mary. On October 13 of that year, thousands of people gathered and claimed they saw the sun dancing in the sky. Newspaper accounts even describe how clothes and puddles that had been soaked with rain earlier had become completely dry. Skeptics can't deny that a group claimed to see this miracle because of these contemporary reports, which leaves even atheists like Richard Dawkins saying, "It is not easy to explain how 70,000 people could share the same hallucination."[66]

To give another example, in 2024, Travis Dumsday released an academic study of the Marian apparition in Zeitoun,

Egypt, in 1968, where possibly millions of people, including non-Christians like Muslims, saw what appeared to be the Virgin Mary above a church in the city. There are even photographs of the apparitions, and the illuminated figure continued to appear even though authorities turned off electricity to the area.

And it's not just Marian apparitions. In 2024, Carlos Eire published with Yale University Press a massive history of saints who were witnessed levitating, called *They Flew: A History of the Impossible*. Michael Gross's 2015 book *The Man Who Could Fly: St. Joseph of Copertino and the Mystery of Levitation* chronicles thirty years' worth of sources about this levitating seventeenth-century friar that are not easy to dismiss. Even skeptics admit that the accounts are not legends, and many people thought they saw Joseph levitate, to which the skeptics say . . . maybe he stood on his toes![67]

There are also numerous cases of miracles involving the Eucharist where the bread turned into actual human flesh when it was consecrated, as recounted in Joan Carrol Cruz's book *Eucharistic Miracles* and Franco Serafini's *A Cardiologist Examines Jesus: The Stunning Science Behind Eucharistic Miracles* (2021). Cruz has written another book on Catholic saints called *incorruptibles*, whose bodies do not decompose as human beings are supposed to after death. Some of the body parts of these saints, called relics, have also been witnessed to effect things like miraculous healings. St. Augustine said there were so many stories of relics healing the sick and holy men raising the dead that he apologized to his readers for being unable to record them all. Augustine even describes the healing of a blind man that happened in the city where he lived.[68]

In the *Summa Contra Gentiles*, St. Thomas Aquinas says miracles were more common in Scripture because their testimony was needed to establish God's covenants. They were less common later in Christian history, but not unheard of, and Aquinas even cites later miracles as evidence for the truth of Catholicism: "Yet it is also a fact that, even in our own time, God does not cease to work miracles through his saints for the confirmation of the Faith."[69]

The Problem of Competing Miracles

So how could a Protestant respond to claims of Catholic miracles validating the Catholic Church's message of salvation?

One approach is to deny that these events occurred at all. John Calvin called some of these accounts "frivolous and ridiculous, so vain and false."[70] In 1918, Calvinist author B.B. Warfield published a book called *Counterfeit Miracles*, in which he said, "The worldview of the Catholic is one all his own and is very expressly a miraculous one. He reckons with the miraculous in every act; miracle suggests itself to him as a natural explanation of every event; and nothing seems too strange to him to be true." Warfield dismissed medieval Catholic miracle stories coming from "the thought of an age so little instructed in the true character of the forces of nature, and especially its deeply seated conception of the essentially magical nature of religion and its modes of working."[71]

But honest Protestants have pointed out how this dismissive skepticism undermines evidence for Christianity itself. Phillip Barnes says of Warfield, "If the same considerations adduced by Warfield in his dismissal of post-apostolic miracles were applied to some biblical stories, then a similar negative verdict would be required in the latter cases as the former."[72] In the nineteenth century, Cardinal John Henry Newman noted this double standard among Protestant critics of Catholicism:

> When, then, controversialists go through the existing accounts of ecclesiastical miracles, and explain one after another on the hypothesis of natural causes . . . they are but expressing their own disbelief in the grace committed to the Church; and of course they are consistent in denying its outward triumphs, when they have no true apprehension of its inward power.[73]

Some Protestants claim that these miracles should have no force to compel a Protestant to convert because the Catholic Church doesn't demand belief in these miracles. The *Catechism* refers to them as "private revelation" and says, "They do not belong . . . to the deposit of faith. It is not their role to improve or complete Christ's definitive revelation, but to help live more fully by it in a certain period of history" (67).

Now, it's true that we do not have a *moral* duty to believe in the miracles of private revelation, because God did not bind us to accept them as he did with a public revelation like Christ's resurrection. But we still have a *rational* duty not to dismissively reject evidence that would lead us to an obligatory moral belief, like that Christ established the Catholic Church. Newman put it this way concerning the miracles of private revelation over the ages:

> Though not part of the philosophical basis of Christianity, they may be evidence still to those who admit the divine presence in the Church, and in proportion as they realize it; they may be evidence in combination with more explicit miracles, or when viewed all together in their cumulative force; they may confirm or remind of the apostolic miracles; they may startle, they may spread an indefinite awe over certain transactions or doctrines.[74]

Other Protestants will say that if Catholic miracles prove that Catholicism is true, then Protestant miracles prove that Protestantism is true. But most examples of miracles in Protestant contexts are not affirmations of uniquely Protestant doctrines like *sola scriptura* or *sola fide*. Instead, they tend to be things like faith healings, as recorded in Protestant author Craig Keener's 2021 book *Miracles Today*.

Indeed, God could perform a miracle through a non-Catholic Christian to demonstrate the lordship and power of Jesus Christ. A Catholic acknowledging this good work would parallel the following event in Luke's Gospel: "John answered, 'Master, we saw a man casting out demons in your name, and we forbade him, because he does not follow with us.' But Jesus said to him, 'Do not forbid him; for he that is not against you is for you'" (9:49-50).

This is why we should be cautious in interpreting the meaning of any miracle claim. The apparition in Zeitoun occurred at a Coptic Orthodox church, but since the apparition didn't say anything, we have little evidence to consider it an affirmation that Coptic Orthodoxy is the true faith. It may just be an affirmation of the spiritual protection Mary offers to those who seek her intercession, something Catholic and Orthodox agree about.

But in other cases, the message seems fairly tailored to endorse Catholic theology. This includes apparitions saying, "I am the Immaculate Conception," as at Lourdes in 1858, and eucharistic hosts turning into human flesh. Catholic philosophers Tyler McNabb and Joseph Blado make this point as well in the context of events such as Fatima:

> We should expect that if a figure who represents a specific Christian tradition appears, then it would give credence to the truth of that tradition (assuming the figure

> does not denounce said tradition). For instance, if Martin Luther appeared with a message from God, then many would consider this to be evidence that the Protestant tradition is correct over the Roman Catholic tradition. Or if John Calvin showed up with a message from God, then this would serve as evidence that the Reformed Protestant tradition is correct over other Protestant traditions (and Roman Catholicism as well). Likewise, the fact that God chose Mary to reveal his message in a Roman Catholic context, that is, a context where heavy Marian devotion is both common and seen as biblical, gives us evidence that the Roman Catholic tradition is correct.[75]

A Dilemma for the "Pleasant Protestant"

The large number of distinctly Catholic miracles throughout history, including Marian apparitions that some Protestants say are supernatural in nature, should be unsettling to a group of people I call "pleasant Protestants."

Who are they?

Well, they aren't the unpleasant Protestants, who think the Catholic Church teaches a false gospel and so Catholicism damns people to hell. If you have that unpleasant view, then it's quite natural to assume that all Catholic miracles are demonic deceptions that entice people to join a false religion and be damned for all eternity.

But what if you're a more pleasant Protestant? What if you think Catholicism *is* a Christian denomination capable of leading people to salvation but just has theological errors, like any other denomination you don't belong to, and that's the only reason you aren't Catholic? If you think that, then it's odd for you to appeal to the devil being the source of alleged

Catholic miracles; if that were true, then why would the devil be tricking people into joining, from your perspective, a Christian denomination that preaches the gospel and so saves people from hell?

It's sort of like how we say, borrowing from C.S. Lewis, that Jesus can't be a nice man. He is either a liar, a lunatic, or the Lord. But Christ's testimony, holiness, and miracles, like his resurrection, show that he must be Lord. Likewise, the Catholic Church, with its teachings on the Eucharist being the one Christ we adore, the witness of the saints, and the overwhelming amount of Catholic miracles throughout history, can't merely be a "nice church."

Catholicism is either deceptive, demonic, or divine. The wide assortment of different testimonies to miracles over the past 2,000 years, even from non-Catholics, disproves deception. The Church's commitment to the gospel and the Nicene Creed disproves it being "demonic." So this leaves us with divine.

And so, I would encourage Protestants to discern if it would be good for your soul to reject the Church Jesus Christ not only established but has continually vindicated with unique miracles throughout its history.

PART II

Answering Objections to the Catholic View of Salvation

OBJECTION 1

A Gift We Can't Earn

"Salvation is a gift from God. It doesn't involve any works or actions on our part: 'For by grace you have been saved through faith; and this is not your own doing, it is the gift of God—not because of works, lest any man should boast'" (Eph. 2:8-9).

This is probably the most common verse I hear when Protestants explain why they object to the Catholic view of salvation. But it shouldn't be an issue at all, because Catholics agree with everything in Ephesians 2:8-9.

The *Catechism of the Catholic Church* says, "Since the initiative belongs to God in the order of grace, no one can merit the initial grace of forgiveness and justification, at the beginning of conversion" (2010). This means there is *no good work we do* that earns salvation as a due reward (which would be something to boast about!).

Catholics agree with Protestants that a) there is a first moment of our salvation and b) we did nothing to earn the precious gift we received in this moment. Our disagreement is about whether this first moment is the *only* moment of our salvation and whether there is any bad work we could later do to reject God's gift.

Of Salvation and Shipwrecks

We know that the apostle Paul taught that our salvation does not consist of a single moment, because he spoke of salvation as being a past event that has already happened ("saved through faith," as in Ephesians above), *and* as a present event that is happening now (see 1 Cor. 15:1), *and* as a future event that hasn't happened yet (for example, in Romans 13:11, where he says that "salvation is nearer to us now than when we first believed"). In my book *Why We're Catholic*, I compared the process of salvation to people who are rescued from a shipwreck:

> Imagine you are caught in a storm at sea with some friends and your boat is sinking. You hear a broadcast on your radio telling you that if you want to be saved you must put on life jackets, report your position, and wait for help to arrive. As the boat pitches up and down and water sprays over the bow, you reply into the radio, "Yes, save us!" You then put on the life jackets and dive into the water.
>
> Two days go by, and your rescuers are nowhere to be seen. One of your friends says help isn't coming and decides to swim to shore on his own: he is never seen again. A few days later, a rescue boat finds you, pulls you onto the deck, and you breathe a sigh of relief. "Saved!"
>
> But when exactly were you saved? Was it when you set foot on the rescue boat? Or was it when you made the initial radio call? The Bible teaches that salvation is a process that begins in the past through faith, continues throughout our lives in the present, and ends with our future eternal glory in heaven.[76]

In this example, salvation involved more than the first moment of seeking help or the last moment when you reached the safety of shore. It also included all the moments in between these points, in which the shipwreck survivors did not forsake the rescue they freely accepted. No one in this scenario saved himself by his own "works." (And the two people who tried met a tragic end!) This shows that although only God can get us to heaven, we can get ourselves to hell. Paul even describes people who rejected their conscience and, as a result, "made shipwreck of their faith" (1 Tim. 1:19).

I had nothing to boast about when, in the tenth grade, I came to believe that Jesus was my Lord and my God. I was only able to declare that because God gave me the free gift of faith and opened my heart to accepting Christ and his offer of salvation. I could have said no and resisted the Holy Spirit, as the early persecutors of the Church did (Acts 7:51), but through the power of God's grace I cooperated with his Spirit and said yes.

As a sinner, I was more than capable of saying no to God, and so I could have boasted of that! (Perhaps people in hell get a sick pleasure in such a boast.) But I could not boast about saying yes to God any more than a person lost at sea could "boast" about letting a rescue helicopter pick him up. In both cases, the only acceptable response is gratitude.

Once again, Catholics completely agree with what Paul teaches in these verses: by grace we have been saved through faith; and this is not our own doing but the gift of God.

No Accessories Needed

We did nothing to receive the first moment of our salvation. And we do nothing to keep our salvation—in the sense that we do not work to earn our place in heaven. Let me repeat: we do not receive salvation through any kind of good work. The Council of Trent, held in the sixteenth century in the wake of the Protestant Reformation, even quotes Romans 11:6 (which many Protestants use to critique the Church) to underscore this point: "None of those things which precede justification—whether faith or works—merit the grace itself of justification. 'For, if it be a grace, it is not now by works, otherwise, as the same apostle says, grace is no more grace.'"[77]

The first moment of salvation is not earned through any good work. It is offered and accepted as a gift, as I accepted God's movement of faith, and the desire to be baptized, in my teenage heart. This initial salvation comes to us by grace alone and nothing, not even personal faith, merits it. That's why, as we saw in chapter five, that babies are saved in baptism without having a personal faith.

Even after this first moment of salvation we graciously receive, there are no particular deeds a Catholic does to earn final salvation along the way to "heaven's shores." All we must do is remain united to Christ at the moment of death. That's why John 3:36 says, "He who believes in the Son has eternal life; he who does not obey the Son shall not see life, but the wrath of God rests upon him."

In Ephesians 2:10, Paul says, "For we are his workmanship, created in Christ Jesus for good works, which God prepared beforehand, that we should walk in them." This shows that there are good works God wants us to do as his children and there are bad works we must avoid that would cause us to forsake our salvation.

St. Paul even warned the Ephesians to "not grieve the Holy Spirit of God" and that "immoral or impure" men have no inheritance in Christ (5:5). He then applies this warning to his audience: "Let no one deceive you with empty words, for it is because of these things that the wrath of God comes upon the sons of disobedience" (5:6). At the end of his letter, Paul says the Church will be at the final judgment "without spot or wrinkle or any such thing, that she might be holy and blameless" (5:27).

Salvation is not just between "me and Jesus." The Church now ushers in the kingdom of God into the world and this Church will be brought collectively to final salvation. But whether we will still be united to the Church when that happens is not guaranteed. We are still free in this life to "jump ship" from the Barque of Peter. This is why Paul clarifies that Christ will present us "holy and blameless and irreproachable before him, *provided that you continue in the faith*, stable and steadfast, not shifting from the hope of the gospel which you heard" (Col. 1:22-23).

If we disobey Christ, we cannot remain in him or his Church. And if we are not united to Christ through his body the Church, we cannot spend eternity with him in heaven. Protestants are correct that salvation is a free, unmerited gift from God. But they are wrong when they claim this gift cannot be forsaken. "You can't lose a gift you didn't earn in the first place!" they say.

And to that *I* say: tell that to Adam and Eve!

Our first parents did nothing to merit God's friendship in the Garden of Eden, but they were still capable of rejecting God's grace; and we face the same danger if we listen to the voice of the tempter as they did instead of the voice of the Spirit whom God has sent into our hearts to guide us to our final salvation in him.

OBJECTION 2:

You Can't Lose Salvation

"The Catholic view of salvation is wrong, because we do not cause or contribute to our salvation. God is the one who saves us, which means a true Christian can't lose his salvation."

The first formal debate I had with a Protestant was at a conference with 1,200 Calvinists in attendance. We debated the question "Can a true Christian lose his salvation?"

In the debate, I quoted from the Bible, early Christians, and Protestant scholars, including Martin Luther. I showed the audience that my view wasn't merely the "Catholic position" on the issue but the historic Christian view. One Protestant emailed me afterward saying, "Great job on the debate! It almost felt like you gave 'Lutheran Answers' instead of 'Catholic Answers' . . . but I fully agree with what you said!"

Many Protestants agree with Catholics that there are things we must do to remain in Christ, even if they disagree over *what* we must do. In treating these first few objections, however, I'm going to focus on the large number of Protestants, especially Reformed and Evangelical Christians, who claim that after we are saved there is *nothing* we must do to remain in a state of salvation, because salvation cannot be lost. This is the doctrine often called *eternal security*.

Committing Spiritual Adultery

Salvation isn't something we can "lose" like we lose our car keys—in the sense of accidentally misplacing or forgetting it. However, the Bible is clear that you and I can *forsake* our salvation by choosing not to remain in union with Christ. We can do this formally and explicitly, or informally and implicitly, through our actions, inactions, and attitudes.

Historically, even Protestants like Martin Luther, who preached salvation by "faith alone," believed that if a person rejected faith, he would lose his salvation. That's because it was by that faith that he was initially saved and he cannot be saved without faith. Luther said,

> To fall from grace means to lose the atonement, the forgiveness of sins, the righteousness, liberty, and life which Jesus has merited for us by his death and resurrection. To lose the grace of God means to gain the wrath and judgment of God, death, the bondage of the devil, and everlasting condemnation.[78]

Luther is commenting on Galatians 5:4, which condemns Christians who tried to enter heaven by following the Law of Moses—in particular by making circumcision necessary for salvation. Paul says, "You are severed from Christ, you who would be justified by the law; you have fallen away from grace" (Gal. 5:4). These people may have believed in Christ, but they betrayed him through their actions. They united themselves to something else for salvation even though it is through Christ alone we are saved (John 14:6).

Our actions can communicate something true even if we say the opposite with our mouths. Just as a husband can forsake his wife through infidelity, even if he says, "Honey, I still love you," Christians can forsake Christ through serious sin even if they say, "Lord, I still love you." Jesus even gives this chilling warning on the Sermon on the Mount: "Not every one who says to me, 'Lord, Lord,' shall enter the kingdom of heaven, but he who does the will of my Father who is in heaven" (Matt. 7:21).

That doesn't mean salvation is *permanently* lost through sin, since a sinner can repent and be reconciled to Christ just as a philandering husband can repent and be reconciled with his wife. But it does mean we are capable of committing acts that, if not repented-for, cause us to reject Christ—with dire eternal consequences.

Christians who believe in eternal security offer biblical arguments for their position. But before we look at those, let's examine some common *non*-biblical arguments that are given to support that view.

What Is Eternal Life?

One argument is that "eternal life" can only mean just that. How could we say that believers have "eternal life" if it were possible for them to end up in hell later? No, our initial act of faith must mean that we are forever secure in our relationship with Christ. Nothing *we* ever do could change the work he has done in us.

The problem with this argument is that it misunderstands what Scripture means when it says we have "eternal life."

It doesn't just mean immortality, because *all* people will continue to exist forever. Our souls are immortal and after the general resurrection we will receive new immortal bodies. (That's one thing that makes hell so hellish.) Eternal life means a certain *kind* of existence; a life united to Christ.

The late Baptist scholar Dale Moody points out "the false assumption that the adjective 'eternal' is an adverb, as if it says the brother eternally has life." He continues, "It is the *life* that is eternal, not one's possession of it. Eternal life is the life of God in Christ the Son of God, and this life is lost when one departs from Christ."[79]

Christ doesn't "eternally give us life." He gives us "eternal life," which means a life with him. But as we will see in several Scripture passages, we are still free to depart from Christ and thus have unending life *apart from* him.

Another argument says that if salvation could be lost, then *everyone* would lose it, because it's just too hard to stay perfectly united to Christ.

But this assumes that losing our salvation *is* as easy as losing our car keys. However, the Catholic and historic Christian belief is that a sin only becomes mortal—only separates us from Christ—when we freely choose to break God's moral law in a serious way. Most Christians don't casually commit these kinds of sins every day. (See appendix 2 for a way to discern which sins are mortal.)

The argument also implies that once salvation is lost it can never be regained. Yet God calls everyone to regular repentance, including those he has saved. King David had been a friend of God, but then he committed murder and adultery, and thereby separated himself from God's friendship. But afterward he was able to repent of sins and restore—and eventually die in—that friendship.

Missing for 1,500 Years

You should also know that this view is a novelty in the history of biblical interpretation. It was virtually unknown among Christians until the Protestant Reformation in the sixteenth century. There were a *few* unnamed heretics in the early Church who defended the idea, but the early heroes of the

Faith we look up to, such as St. Augustine, rejected it—and no prominent early Christian defended it.[80]

In the second century, St. Irenaeus said that "those who do not obey him being disinherited by him, have ceased to be his sons. Wherefore they cannot receive his inheritance."[81] The third-century writer Tertullian asked, "For do not many afterward fall out of [grace]? Is not this gift taken away from many?"[82] Augustine said that among those who were regenerate and justified (that is, saved Christians), some "because of his own free choice to evil he has lost the grace of God, that he had received."[83]

Peter Lillback, president of the Protestant Westminster Seminary, says,

> The evidence is clear—eternal security was not a doctrine that was carefully considered by the uninspired founding fathers of our Christian tradition. It is hard to believe, but in over 5,000 pages of the Ante-Nicene writings, John 3:16 is only cited twice! . . . There are elements of [the Church Fathers] that can be viewed as moving away from grace toward what Wright has termed an "early Catholicism."[84]

As we discuss passages in Scripture that some Protestants use to defend the idea that salvation cannot be lost, ask yourself why no prominent Christian reached the same conclusion about these passages until 1,500 years into Christian history. Were the apostles just really bad at teaching this important truth to their successors? Or was it because this doctrine isn't an apostolic truth at all?

OBJECTION 3:

All Sin Is Equally Bad

"All sin is sin and makes us unworthy of heaven! The Catholic idea that only some sins are 'mortal' that could cause us to lose salvation contradicts the Bible's teaching that Jesus saves us from all sin."

When Protestants hear about "mortal" and "venial" sin, they might be tempted to conclude that, according to this Catholic distinction, if unbelievers only committed venial sins in life, they would still go to heaven. But these categories only apply to Christians. Unbaptized persons, still in a state of original sin, cannot enter heaven just by the work of avoiding mortal sins. They still lack the *sanctifying grace* that puts them in friendship with God and makes them capable of receiving their heavenly rewards.

For Christians, venial sins damage our relationship with God but mortal sins sever that relationship. They involve a complete turning away from God and his gift of salvation. These sins happen when a person freely and knowingly chooses to engage in a serious act of evil.

In my experience, although Protestants may not use the terms *mortal* and *venial* they absolutely believe there are different kinds of sins and that each affects us in different ways. They don't *really* believe that "sin is sin" or that "all sins are equal before God." We can know this by asking two questions:

- Do Christians have to confess to God every individual sin they commit?
- Are there any individual sins that Christians *must* confess to God?

Big Sin and Little Sins

Let's start with the first question. Do we have to confess to God *every* individual sin we commit?

Most Christians would agree that the answer is no. We don't have to expressly pray, "Lord, please forgive me for my impatience with Frank at 10:30 a.m., my act of gossip with Marge at 10:40, my indecent curiosity at 10:45," and so on. We may include such sins generally when we make an examination of conscience, or in the Lord's Prayer when we ask God to "forgive us our trespasses," but we don't spell them all out specifically, day after day.

James 3:2 says we all stumble in many small ways. We all commit what can be called minor sins, but we don't consider such sins to be a sign that a person isn't a true Christian or expect Christians to ask God to forgive each one by name.

But many Protestants would answer yes to the second question. There *are* sins that are so serious we must ask God to forgive them by name.

The Christian husband, for example, who commits adultery and then confronts his guilt, doesn't just say the Lord's Prayer and consider the matter resolved. Deep down, serious Christians know that serious sins require a deliberate response. We ask God to specially forgive serious sins—*mortal* sins—apart from the minor sins we commit every day.

And it's not just the act, but the circumstances of the sin that make a difference.

Most Christians don't think we must confess to God every single white lie we tell, but we should confess if one of our lies got someone fired or imprisoned for a crime he didn't commit. We don't have to confess eating an extra chocolate-covered almond straight out of the barrel of the grocery store without paying for it, but we should confess stealing money from elderly widows that decimates their life savings. One example of lying and one example of stealing is vastly more serious than the other, and so those sins are not equal before God.

This is so obvious, in fact, that if you treated plundering widows or perjury that falsely imprisons someone as lightly as stealing a single piece of candy, most Protestants would say you were never saved in the first place!

Repentant vs. Unrepentant?

One might object that the real distinction isn't between major and minor sins, but sins for which we are *repentant* versus *unrepentant*. If a person committed even a small sin continually and didn't feel sorry about it, he could not have been saved.

Let's reflect on this by considering two Christians: Dave and Denny. Dave uses his parents' Netflix password every few months even though this constitutes stealing per Netflix's terms of service. Dave knows this, but he doesn't think it's a big deal. And then there's Denny, who commits murder every few months but also doesn't think it's a big deal.

Denny isn't purely hypothetical. A man named Dennis Rader was a Cub Scout leader and president of the council at his Lutheran church . . . until he was arrested in 2005 and later convicted of ten murders. During his time of leadership at the church, he savagely and ritualistically killed several young women, becoming known as the "BTK"—bind, torture, and kill—killer.

Let's go further and say that Dave and Denny both commit their sins without repentance not every couple of months, but only once a year, and only across a single decade. Most Protestants who believe salvation can't be lost would say that Denny's killing spree was proof that he was never saved. But if *lack of repentance* were all that mattered, they would have to say the same thing about Dave's annual act of Netflix-sneaking—or any other minor sin for which someone is unrepentant.

Aside from the moral perversity of equating murder with petty theft, this approach to sin would create a practical nightmare for believers. Jesus said, "My yoke is easy, my burden is light" (Matt. 11:30)—but what could be more burdensome than having to muster the same penitence for *every single sin* you commit, whether it's homicide or haughtiness?

What makes more sense is that some sins, by their very nature, are so serious that their natural effect is a complete rejection of God and his salvation. Whereas other sins are not as serious; and so, even when they are committed repeatedly or without our express repentance, they damage our relationship with God but don't destroy it. As 1 John 5:17 says, "All wrongdoing is sin, but there is sin which is not mortal."

One Part = the Whole Law?

What about James 2:10, which says, "Whoever keeps the whole law but fails in one point has become guilty of all of it"? Doesn't that mean that there is no such thing as a difference mortal and venial sin because committing *any* sin is equal to committing *every* sin?

Note that James is not saying all sins are equally *wrong*. In the previous nine verses he scolds Christians who show favoritism and choose which men to love (the rich) and which men not to love (the poor). He says, "If you really fulfil the royal law, according to the Scripture, "You shall love your neighbor as yourself," you do well. But if you show partiality, you commit sin, and are convicted by the law as transgressors" (James 2:8-9).

Christians are saved by grace but still live under a moral law. This is what James calls the "royal law" and Paul calls "the law of Christ" in Galatians 6:2. Christians don't get to pick and choose who they must love and which moral laws they must follow. That's why James then says, "For whoever keeps the whole law but fails in one point has become guilty of all of it. For he who said, 'Do not commit adultery,' said also, 'Do not kill.' If you do not commit adultery but do kill, you have become a transgressor of the law."

In other words, a Christian can't tell God, "So what if I hated my neighbor? At least I loved a bunch of other people!" just as he can't say, "So what if I murdered a guy? At least I didn't sleep with his wife!"

The fact that a person keeps some major parts of the moral law (like not committing adultery) doesn't excuse his failure to keep other major parts of the law (like not murdering). Jesus even recognized that some people who break minor parts of the law will still go to heaven when he said, "Whoever then relaxes one of the least of these commandments and teaches men so, shall be called least in the kingdom of heaven" (Matt. 5:19).

Some Protestants balk at the idea of Christians being under any "law," since they believe that Christ did away with laws. Yet this is not the case. It's true that Christ did away with the Law of Moses, the Law of the Old Covenant, but the New Testament says we are under a new law in Christ.

Pharisee or "Fair, I See"

Some Protestants might say we're being legalistic—trying to parse out *just* the serious sins as if those were the only ones we needed to avoid. They'd say that instead of imitating the Pharisees in this way, we should just trust in Jesus' radical call to holiness.

This is correct in one sense. The person who indulges in venial sins while legalistically avoiding mortal sins is playing Russian roulette with his soul. God spoke through the prophet Isaiah of these kinds of men "who honor me with their lips, while their hearts are far from me" (29:13). People who only worry about mortal sins are engaged in the sin of *presumption*: thinking their minor sins won't catch up to them and dispose them toward the fatal choice to do something really evil. Grave acts of theft, adultery, and murder are almost always preceded by numerous instances of less grave, but still sinful, acts—petty theft, lustful looks, hateful anger—that damage our moral compass.

But it is incorrect in another sense. It's important to know which sins sever our relationship with God and which sins just injure it so that we can respond appropriately. For example, if you were bitten by a snake, you would probably want to know if it's the kind of bite that just causes pain and requires a little ice and rest or if it's a bite that contains venom that can kill you if you don't get treatment fast. And to know the difference, you'd need a specific list (see the list in this book's conclusion for a start).

That's why we're going to continue our focus on one crucial point that bridges the divide between Catholics and many Protestants when it comes to salvation: it is possible for a true Christian to commit a grave evil that results in him forsaking God's free gift of salvation.

OBJECTION 4:

Jesus Won't Let Go!

"You can't lose your salvation because Jesus promised he would lose none of those whom the Father gave him."

"Jesus has got you in his hand, and he ain't gonna let you go! That's how you know you have assurance. That's how you know you have eternal life!"

Many people in the crowd nodded their heads in approvement at this street preacher, but I was skeptical. The preacher then began to read from Scripture:

"'My sheep hear my voice, and I know them, and they follow me; and I give them eternal life, and they shall never perish, and no one shall snatch them out of my hand' (John 10:27-28). You see, folks? The Lord says, '*No one* is able to snatch you out of the Father's hand!'"

Then a young man in the crowd piped up: "But couldn't you leave Jesus' hand yourself?" I had been thinking the same thing. The pastor strolled over to him.

"Son, give me your hand."

He reluctantly did.

"Now, try to walk away."

The young man tried but the pastor, smiling through a big bushy beard, yanked the young man's arm right back and then broke into a laugh.

"You see, nobody can snatch you out of my hand because I got you tight. And the same is true with the Lord. The Father gave us to him and none of us are going anywhere. Praise the Lord!"

Who Are Christ's Sheep?

We've already seen that "eternal" life means a kind of life shared with Jesus, not a life that can't be lost. Jesus promises that no one can ever take this shared life away from us. Yet Jesus does not promise that *we* will never forsake him. The passages used to argue that Christians can't lose their salvation, then, are talking about the security of those who *presently* remain in Christ.

Consider the verse my preacher friend expounded: "My sheep hear my voice, and I know them, and they follow me." Those who profess eternal security read the verse and think that what makes someone a follower of Christ is his status as one of Christ's sheep. Once you get saved and become one of Christ's sheep, you will always be part of his flock.

But this is a backward reading. The promise is about *believers in the present* who choose to continue following Christ. It is not being one of the sheep that makes us a follower of Christ—it is being a follower of Christ that makes us one of the sheep.

We did not choose to follow Christ on our own—he called us to himself first—but we do choose to continue to follow Christ. And we will know whether we currently belong to Christ's flock or whether we have gone astray by how we listen to his voice. This can be seen in John 6:40, when Jesus says, "For this is the will of my Father, that every one who sees the Son and believes in him should have eternal life; and I will raise him up at the last day."

Notice that Jesus is using *present tense* verbs. Jesus is not saying that everyone who *ever believed* in him will have eternal life. As the Reformed apologist James White admits, "The wonderful promises that are provided by Christ are not for those who do not truly and continuously believe."[85]

This also answers those who argue that 1 John 5:13 says we can't forsake our salvation because it promises that "you who believe in the name of the Son of God . . . know that you have eternal life." For John, belief isn't just a onetime mental acceptance of facts about Christ. And good deeds are not an automatic or accidental byproduct of faith. Instead, our keeping the commandments shows *that we truly believe.* Earlier in that same letter, John writes,

> Every one who believes that Jesus is the Christ is a child of God, and every one who loves the parent loves the child. By this we know that we love the children of God, when we love God and obey his commandments. For this is the love of God, that we keep his commandments. And his commandments are not burdensome (1 John 5:1-3).

John says that we're able to know we have eternal life because *we can know we are in Christ by observing our own actions.* And, provided we remain in Christ, we will spend eternity with him. This doesn't mean we have to be perfect, because John also says, "If we say we have no sin, we deceive ourselves, and the truth is not in us" (1 John 1:8). It just means we must not remain in grave sin that separates us from Christ and causes the loss of eternal life. As John explains, "All wrongdoing is sin, but there is sin which is not mortal" (1 John 5:17).

If we are in a state of mortal sin, we are not currently united to Christ and so we must repent, receive Christ, and ask for his grace to remain united with him until death.

Who Can Jesus Lose?

Didn't Jesus say, "This is the will of him who sent me, that I should lose nothing of all that he has given me, but raise it up at the last day" (John 6:39)? If a true Christian could end up in hell, wouldn't that mean Jesus failed to do the Father's will?

To answer that, we need to understand the *active* and *permissive* aspects of God's will. God directly causes some things to happen, but other things God simply *allows* to happen in accord with his divine plan for the universe. For example, God hates sin (Prov. 6:16–20) and so God never actively wills for us to sin. But our sins don't catch God by surprise. He *allows* us to sin; and, since everything God allows may be called an expression of his will, it may be said that our sins are part of what we call God's *permissive* will. He permits such evils in order to allow greater goods to exist: such as the freedom to choose good or evil, which is the freedom to choose to love God or reject him.

Notice also that Jesus says it is God's will that *his son* not lose any who were given to him. Jesus will not lose us, but that doesn't mean *we* can't lose Jesus. That's why St. John Chrysostom said in the fourth century that Jesus meant, "At least *for my part*, I will not lose them" [emphasis added]. Jesus even says that the Father gave him all the apostles to guard, yet one of them *was* lost—"the son of perdition" (John 17:12). Jesus did not "lose" a single person the Father gave him, but he did allow his betrayer, Judas Iscariot, to reject him and "go to his own place" (Acts 1:25).[86]

Chrysostom goes on to say that Jesus, "declaring the matter more clearly, said, 'I will not reject anyone who comes to me,'" which is a reference to John 6:37: "All that the Father gives me will come to me; and him who comes to me I will not cast out."

Once again: Christ will never lose us or reject us. But that doesn't mean we cannot do the same to him. When I used to visit a professor at my old college, I knew he would never kick me out of his office when I came to see him during office hours. However, I was free to leave whenever I liked. Protestant scholar Ben Witherington says that in John's Gospel,

> We are not told here that someone God draws, or even Jesus chooses, may not commit apostasy or rebellion . . . Even though the Fourth Gospel has a strong view of God's sovereignty, it also recognizes that there are things that happen that are contrary to God's desires and will.[87]

Rejection Is a One-Way Street

Finally, there's John 6:44: "No one can come to me unless the Father who sent me draws him; and I will raise him up at the last day." Those who quote this passage say the Father gives the saved to Jesus and Jesus then takes this same group of people all the way to heaven. There's simply no chance for them to fall away, because at all times they are in some form of divine custody.

However, Jesus' teaching here is a contrast between God's ability to save us and man's inability to save himself. No one can come to Jesus solely through his own human abilities. He must be drawn by the Father. And no one can raise himself to heaven because we love sin too much to do that. Instead, Jesus must raise us up to heaven.

In a similar contrast, whereas we can only approach Christ through the Father's grace, we can reject Christ all on our own, through our sins. As we will see in the next section, Jesus makes this clear in his other teachings when he gives specific warnings about those who receive grace from him and the Father but then reject it and suffer eternal consequences.

OBJECTION 5:

They Were False Believers

"When the Bible talks about 'falling away,' it's referring to false believers: people who were never true Christians to begin with. A true Christian can never lose his salvation."

"I can't believe he isn't even Christian anymore . . ."

I was surprised, but only for a moment, because I'd heard this story so many times.

In my early college years, I used to debate the radical views on dating held by a popular Protestant author that were all the rage among certain conservative and homeschooled Christians. That author even held up as an ideal that young people should refrain from kissing until marriage. Twenty years later (ten of which I spent blissfully married and free from the anxieties of dating life) I was shocked to see this author had completely changed his tune.

However, he didn't just rebuke what he said about dating. He said he didn't even believe in Jesus anymore.

As I said, I'd heard this story so many times. On my podcast I once interviewed a well-known Christian musician who abandoned his faith. Some of the atheists I've formally debated, like Dan Barker, used to be Christian pastors. So when some Protestants tell me it's impossible to forsake salvation, I point to these former Christians and ask for an explanation. And what I get is always the same: "They were never actually saved in the first place."

Counterfeit Conversions?

In the first letter of the apostle John, he describes "antichrists" who "went out from us, but they were not of us; for if they had been of us, they would have continued with us; but they went out, that it might be plain that they all are not of us" (1 John 2:19).

I agree that some people who become Christian underwent a false conversion. They may have never believed in Jesus at all; or their motives were bad; or they had only a superficial or incomplete faith in Christ; or maybe they believed in a false "Jesus" of their own making. But just because *some* former Christians (apostates) had a corrupted faith from the start that doesn't mean that *all* of them did.

Moreover, the common explanation, "They were never saved in the first place," when used in defense of eternal security, ironically *robs* people of the security they should have in their status as children of God.

Some Protestants think that the possibility of losing salvation constantly hangs over our heads as Catholics, keeping us in a waking nightmare that we're always one wrong move away from damnation. But as we've noted, Catholics don't keep a ledger of good versus bad deeds to earn heaven, and mortal sins aren't something a believer casually commits.

It's true that the Bible says we have "peace with God" (Rom. 5:1), but that doesn't mean peace can never be broken. The United States and Japan have had peace since the end of World War II, but that peace wouldn't last long if the United States dropped another atomic bomb on Japan. And that's what mortal sins are: atomic bombs that destroy the love of God in our souls.

Catholics can examine their consciences, review their deeds, discern the state of their souls, and seek to repent of these "nuclear" sins. But Protestants who believe in eternal security can't. All they can do is conclude that serious sins mean they weren't saved in the first place.

Some Protestants will use the word *backsliding* to refer to saved Christians who commit serious sins but later repent. Despite those sins, it turns out these people *were* saved in the first place, as demonstrated by their subsequent repentance. But this doesn't really solve the problem, since no one knows whether he will repent of future sins before he dies and thus prove that he was "saved" all along.

Do you see how nerve-wracking it would be to base the legitimacy of your past, supposedly unlosable salvation on what you may or may not do in the future?

I've had countless Protestants friends tell me how they agonized over their initial conversions. Some of them gave their life to Christ when they were adolescents or even children. Then, as adults, they found themselves habitually committing serious sexual sins or doubting their faith entirely. They worried: *Was I truly saved in the first place? Do I have to commit my life to Christ all over again?*

Even those who felt secure in Christ, free from major sin, still had doubts. How could they know they weren't like other apostates who had once believed they were saved? On the outside, those people showed all the fruits of the Holy Spirit and they were free from any scandal. If *they* could deceive themselves into a false sense of eternal security, couldn't anyone?

That's why I am so grateful that Christ's promises of salvation are not for those who *once* followed him or once heard his voice, but for those who *continuously* follow him and seek out his voice always. And if we as sheep ever do go astray, the good shepherd will do anything, even leaving behind the ninety-nine faithful sheep, to come after us. But he won't force us back into the sheepfold, as Jesus' own words make terrifyingly clear.

Those Who Remain and Endure

In John 15:6, Jesus says, "If a man does not abide in me, he is cast forth as a branch and withers; and the branches are gathered, thrown into the fire and burned." The word *abide* comes from a Greek word that just means "stay, remain." In John 10:40, a version of the word refers to Jesus "staying" or remaining across the Jordan before he raised Lazarus from the dead.

Sometimes when you garden you see dead twigs in brush that aren't connected to the vine. To keep the vine healthy, these dead branches need to be cleared away. But those aren't the kind of branches Jesus is talking about. Those dead twigs can never produce fruit.

Jesus is saying that we can produce spiritual fruit if we *remain* in him. He's not talking about people who were never true believers (the dead twigs lying on the brush). He's talking about former believers who have spiritually died because they separated themselves from the vine. They are withered, cut-off branches that were once connected to the vine. That's why Jesus says, "Every branch of mine that bears no fruit, he takes away, and every branch that does bear fruit he prunes, that it may bear more fruit."

My favorite parable that illustrates the possibility of forsaking salvation is the tale of the unforgiving servant in Matthew 18. A servant with a debt he couldn't possibly repay pleads to the king for mercy and it is granted: the debt is forgiven. But later, the servant encounters another servant who owed him a much smaller debt and asks for similar mercy. But instead of showing his fellow servant the royal mercy he had already received, the unmerciful servant has the other servant thrown in jail. This enrages the king, who summons the unmerciful servant to his presence: "You wicked servant! I forgave you all that debt because you besought me; and should not you have had mercy on your fellow servant, as I had mercy on you?" (vv. 32–33).

In the next verse, Jesus tells us, "And in anger his lord delivered him to the jailers, till he should pay all his debt. So also my heavenly Father will do to every one of you, if you do not forgive your brother from your heart."

The servant's debt had been forgiven, but then it was reinstated after his evil behavior. The debt is symbolic of our sins, which is why we ask God the Father to forgive us our "debts" against him as being symbolic of moral trespasses (Matt. 6:12). So again we see that Jesus isn't talking about people who were never true Christians to begin with. The wicked servant was a real servant whose master had forgiven his debt. But then he gravely sinned and incurred punishment as a result.

That's why Jesus solemnly tells us, "You will be hated by all for my name's sake. But he who endures to the end will be saved" (Matt. 10:22).

OBJECTION 6:

It's Paid in Full!

"There is nothing we have to do after being saved, because Jesus said on the cross, 'It is finished!' All of our sins—past, present, and future—have been paid, so there is nothing left for us to do."

After graduating college, I led a group of undergraduate students on a pro-life mission trip to California. In the mornings I would teach them how to use devices like surveys or response tables to create dialogue with strangers on the issue of abortion (no easy feat among tourists who just want to relax).

Afternoons I took the students out and they'd strike up dozens of conversations with total strangers, many of whom began to change their minds on the issue. Since I knew how tough it is engage in this kind of activism, I wanted to treat them to a special dinner afterward.

We arrived at a fancy seaside resort restaurant and met a wealthy friend of mine who lived, not just in a gated neighborhood, but a neighborhood that has an armed, 24/7 security guard posted at the community entrance. The students, many of whom were used to a diet of ramen noodles and energy drinks, became nervous looking at a menu with entrees costing more than some of their textbooks.

The host assured them, "It's all paid for, kids. Get whatever you want!"

Still, they were nervous when the waiter approached.

"Is it okay if I get . . . ?"

"Trent, would it be all right if I ordered . . . ?"

Finally, I blurted out, "Guys, just relax. It's all been paid for. You can stop worrying and just say thank you for the meal!"

I share this story because I often hear Protestants speak about Christ generously paying for all our sins, past, present, and future, in the same way. This means that there is nothing we need to worry about—nothing we must do in order to remain in union with Christ and be saved. But I find that Protestants often didn't act like they believe this, because they still ask for forgiveness on the rare occasions when they commit really serious sins. They are like the students who still felt like they had to ask for their expensive meals to be paid.

Indeed, in this way they reveal how they misunderstand Christ's sacrifice; how it was even more generous than they realize.

Paid in Full?

First it must be noted that Christ's statement "It is finished" (John 19:30) does not literally mean "It is paid in full." That may be a *truth we could glean* from the passage, but it is incorrect to say we can translate the word *tetelestai* in John 19:30 as "paid in full." It's a form of the Greek word *teleō*, which just means to "end" or "finish."

The idea that *tetelestai* means "paid in full" is actually something of an urban legend in biblical exegesis. It came from scholars who noted that receipts from around the time of the New Testament had the Greek word *tetel* stamped on them, indicated they were paid. But this is an abbreviation, and there are five different Greek words that begin with these letters. One of them is *tetelōnētai*, which is a different word from *tetelestai*. It literally means "tax," or "paid as taxes," and it can be found on artifacts of dozens of ancient receipts, where it refers to a tax that has been paid.

The word *tetelestai,* on the other hand, is used in ancient Greek sources to describe finishing artwork or manufacturing, not paying debts. In the New Testament the root word *teleō* is only used for payments in Matthew 17:24 and Romans 13:6, where is doesn't talk about something "paid in full" but paying taxes.

So, if Jesus didn't mean "paid in full," then what did he mean when he said, "It is finished"? One prominent interpretation is that Jesus meant the Old Testament prophecies about the Messiah were now fulfilled in his sacrificial death. Read the preceding verses, which describe what happened after Jesus entrusted his mother to the apostle John:

> After this Jesus, knowing that all was now finished [*tetelestai*], said (to fulfil [*teleiōthē*] the scripture), "I thirst." A bowl full of vinegar stood there; so they put a sponge full of the vinegar on hyssop and held it to his mouth. When Jesus had received the vinegar, he said, "It is finished"; and he bowed his head and gave up his spirit.

John 19:28 is the only other place where *tetelestai* is used in Scripture, and when it's combined with the related word *teleiōthē*, we see the context is related to finishing, completing, or fulfilling messianic prophecies of the Old Testament.

Jesus could also have been referring to the "finishing" of the Last Supper. Jesus did not drink from the fourth cup of the Passover meal. Instead, Jesus refused to drink wine until he came into his kingdom and, then before dying, he drank sour wine on the cross. Catholic theologian Scott Hahn says, "It was the Passover that was now finished. More precisely, it was Jesus' transformation of the Passover sacrifice of the Old Covenant into the eucharistic sacrifice of the New Covenant."[88]

But we can know from a logical perspective and not just a biblical one that these words of Jesus are not about all our sins "being paid for" such that salvation no longer requires cooperation with God's grace.

Salvation Purchased for All?

If all our sins were forgiven on the cross, why did Jesus say that each day we should ask for the Father to "forgive us our trespasses as we forgive those who trespass against us"? Normally, we get annoyed if we forgive someone of an offense and he keeps asking for forgiveness. We want people to take us at our word, like my wealthy friend who meant it when he said, "Order whatever you want!"

Saying that all our sins are paid for but still asking forgiveness for each one would be like if I said to a friend, "All your meals in the dining hall this semester are paid for, past, present, and future," and he kept asking me every single day afterward, "Can you please pay for today's lunch for me?"

The problem with these Protestants is not that they overvalue Christ's sacrifice; it's that they *under*value it. Christ didn't just pay for the past, present, and future sins of believers—those who are called "members of the elect" (the ones God knew would be among the saved). Christ's death on the cross paid for the past, present, and future sins of *every single human being*—including those who would eventually reject Christ and be lost for all eternity. This is why you can tell *anyone* you meet, "Christ died for you." 1 John 2:2 says that Jesus "is the expiation for our sins, and not for ours only but also for the sins of the whole world."

But just because Christ's death "paid for," or atoned for, our sins does not mean that everything about our salvation was finished after Christ died on the cross. Our Lord himself "did things" for our salvation after his crucifixion. For example, we know that Christ's resurrection justifies us because

Romans 4:24-25 speaks of "Jesus our Lord, who was put to death for our trespasses and raised for our justification." St. Paul likewise says, "If Christ has not been raised, your faith is futile and you are still in your sins" (1 Cor. 15:17).

What separates the saved from the damned, whom Christ also died for and whom the Father also wants to save, must be their *response* to God's grace.

As we saw in previous chapters, Jesus taught that God will forgive the debt incurred by our sins, but this debt can also be reinstated if we reject God's mercy. That's why Hebrews 10:26-27 says, "If we sin deliberately after receiving the knowledge of the truth, there no longer remains a sacrifice for sins, but a fearful prospect of judgment." What kind of judgment? The sacred author gives this warning:

> A man who has violated the law of Moses dies without mercy at the testimony of two or three witnesses. How much worse punishment do you think will be deserved by the man who has spurned the Son of God, and profaned the blood of the covenant by which he was sanctified, and outraged the Spirit of grace? (vv. 28-29).

Notice that this is talking about a saved Christian, someone who was "sanctified by the blood of the covenant." The punishment for this person who spurns the Son of God will be worse than the punishment for those rejected God in the Old Testament. Their punishment was death, but those who reject Christ—including those who once accepted him and were sanctified by his blood—will suffer eternal death.

This shows that our justification, and even the act of remitting our sins, was *not* finished when Jesus said "It is finished" on the cross. Our salvation was bought with Christ's blood, but we must still say yes to God to apply that sacrifice to our souls and not reject it after it has been applied.

OBJECTION 7:

The Thief on the Cross Shows Us the Way

"Works have nothing to do with our salvation because Jesus told the good thief on the cross, 'Today, you will be with me in paradise.' He didn't have to do a single good work, and neither do we. All we must do is imitate him and trust in Jesus Christ alone for our salvation."

The Gospels record how Jesus was crucified between two thieves, and in Luke 23 the Evangelist specifically mentions how one of these criminals rebukes the other, saying, "Do you not fear God, since you are under the same sentence of condemnation? And we indeed justly; for we are receiving the due reward of our deeds; but this man has done nothing wrong."

He said to Jesus, "Remember me when you come in your kingly power." And Jesus said to him, "Truly, I say to you, today you will be with me in paradise."

What is most striking to me about the "good thief" was the courage it took for him to say this to Jesus. After all, he had just been *reviling* Jesus. Mark observes, "Those who were crucified with him also reviled him" (15:32), and Matthew says, "the robbers who were crucified with him also reviled him in the same way" (27:44).

If God can work in the hearts of even the vilest sinners, those who would mock Jesus Christ to his face, think of what he can do in our hearts when we mock Christ with our own sins!

However, some Protestants take away a different lesson from this encounter. They claim that Jesus' words to the thief show that a person only needs to trust in Christ to be saved. They say the good thief wasn't baptized and never did any good works, and yet he went to heaven with Christ. Therefore, we can go to heaven by simply having the same kind of faith.

Ordinary and Extraordinary Salvation

Remember how I described the Catholic plan of salvation? Repent, receive, and remain. Well, the good thief on the cross did all three.

First, he *repented* of his sins. The Greek word we translate "repentance" is *metanoia* (the verb "to repent" is *metanoeo*) and it means "to change one's mind." *Metanoia*'s Hebrew counterpart is *tshuva*, which means "to return." God told the people of Israel, "Repent and turn away from your idols; and turn away your faces from all your abominations" (Ezek. 14:6).

In Scripture, *metanoia* refers to changing one's mind about the goodness of sin and abandoning sin in favor of the goodness of God. When Jesus said "repent [*metanoeite*], and believe in the gospel" (Mark 1:15) he is basically saying, "Change your mind about sin and return to God by believing the good news."

Even though we do not hear the man apologize for his sins, it seems clear he has turned away from them. Moreover, the good thief *received* Jesus and then he *remained* united to Christ until his death. Sure, the "remain" portion was a short amount of earthly time, but that's why Jesus says even faith as small as a mustard seed can bloom into a mighty tree of faith (Matt. 17:20) and that even the vineyard workers who work the shortest amount of time will receive the same payment (Matt. 20:1-16).

The thief did not receive Christ through baptism, but he was in the unique position of receiving Jesus in his very midst. He received Jesus in an extraordinary way, whereas we receive him in a way that is more ordinary but no less real. The apostle Thomas proclaimed Jesus as Lord and God after seeing his resurrected body with his eyes, but that doesn't mean a person can only be justified in saying this under those same conditions! In fact, Jesus said to him, "Have you believed because you have seen me? Blessed are those who have not seen and yet believe" (John 20:29).

So, we have to distinguish the *ordinary* ways God saves people from the *extraordinary* ways.

For example, many Protestants believe that the ordinary way we are saved is through faith in Christ. But does that mean everyone without faith is damned? Most Protestants believe that small children and the mentally handicapped who die can still go to heaven even if they never had faith in Christ. If such people are unbaptized, their salvation can't be because they are sinless, because they still suffer from original sin.

None of us, not even a baby, can merit heaven on our own. It is only through God's gracious gift that any human being can have eternal life. But Protestants would reject any argument that says infants who are saved without personal faith means that such faith isn't necessary for *anyone's* salvation. They'd point out that what God does in extraordinary cases of salvation does not overturn the commands he gave for ordinary cases involving people, like you or me, who can hear his offer of salvation and accept or reject it.

The Greatest "Good Work" of All

Nearly all Protestants would deny that in order to be saved we *only* need to have what the good thief had. For example, it's almost certain that the good thief did not believe that God was a Trinity of three persons, Father, Son, and Holy Spirit. He may not have even known Jesus was God incarnate, seeing him instead as God's messenger who would oversee the messianic kingdom.

However, the thief's salvation in spite of these deficiencies would not make belief in the Trinity or the divinity of Christ optional or merely incidental to our salvation. Likewise, the thief's salvation apart from baptism would not make baptism unrelated to our salvation. As the *Catechism* teaches:

> The Lord himself affirms that baptism is necessary for salvation. He also commands his disciples to proclaim the gospel to all nations and to baptize them. Baptism is necessary for salvation for those to whom the gospel has been proclaimed and who have had the possibility of asking for this sacrament. The Church does not know of any means other than baptism that assures entry into eternal beatitude; this is why she takes care not to neglect the mission she has received from the Lord to see that all who can be baptized are "reborn of water and the Spirit." God has bound salvation to the sacrament of baptism, but he himself is not bound by his sacraments (1257).

Because God is all-powerful, he can save people in any way he chooses. But that doesn't give us the right to decide that we can be saved in any way *we* choose.

Finally, one aspect of the good thief's salvation perfectly corresponds to the Catholic plan of salvation: he remained with Christ.

The good thief did what every person does in the ordinary course of salvation—he did not persist in sin but persisted in a state of friendship with God until death. The thief may not have fed the poor or practiced pious prayerful devotion, but he did the greatest work of all: he publicly proclaimed the goodness of Christ, and even rebuked those who scoffed in the Lord's face, before fully entrusting himself to God for his salvation and remaining with him until his painful last breath on the cross.

OBJECTION 8:

Paul Teaches Perfect Assurance

"The man who wrote most of the New Testament says our salvation cannot be lost."

Just as Jesus said no one can snatch us out of his hands, the apostle Paul preaches that the all-powerful God has conquered sin, and so nothing can separate us from him. He puts this eloquently in Romans 8:38-39: "For I am sure that neither death, nor life, nor angels, nor principalities, nor things present, nor things to come, nor powers, nor height, nor depth, nor anything else in all creation, will be able to separate us from the love of God in Christ Jesus our Lord."

Notice that one thing is missing from this list: sin.

That's strange. Paul frequently describes the effect sin has on us and even spoke about how sinned war within his own body: "I see in my members another law at war with the law of my mind and making me captive to the law of sin which dwells in my members" (Rom. 7:23).

Yet he doesn't include sin in his list of the things that can separate us from the love of God. That's because in his writings Paul frequently warned against persistent, sinful actions that can permanently separate us from God's love.

Who Is the "You"?

When reading Paul's letters, modern readers sometimes mistake the specific messages he gave for the Christians of his time as being for every single Christian throughout Church history. Protestants are aware of this, because almost none of them require women to wear head coverings in church, even though Paul said that "if a woman will not veil herself, then she should cut off her hair" (1 Cor. 11:6). The Catholic Church also recognizes that this was a cultural recommendation on Paul's part that is not universally binding upon all the faithful.[89]

But although nearly all Protestants agree that 1 Corinthians 11:6 was meant for a local community, they don't recognize this in Philippians 1:6, which they often cite in favor of the doctrine of eternal security: "And I am sure that he who began a good work in you will bring it to completion at the day of Jesus Christ."

When my Protestant friend Jon was discussing the Bible with me over a pizza lunch, he casually said, "Yeah, I think I can have hope in my salvation, because Paul says he who began a good work in you will complete it."

I gently interrupted him, "Jon, who is the 'you' in that passage?"

Jon admitted it was the Philippian Christians, but he added that the Bible's messages can apply to all Christians even if the literal sense of the text was meant for specific people. For example, the letter to Philemon teaches us about mercy and compassion even though it was only sent to one of Paul's associates. Or, when Paul says in Galatians 2:20 that Christ "loved me and gave himself for me," the "me" refers to Paul but it's also true for all Christians.

But as I noted regarding 1 Corinthians 11:6, this isn't *always* the case. In Philippians 1:6, the hope Paul has is grounded in the Philippians' uniquely holy demeanor. That's why he says he is sure, or in Greek "persuaded" (*pepoithos*), of this truth. Paul was confident they would persevere to final salvation because of how they previously lived out their faith, especially in regard to him. In fact, you can tell that Paul has a special affection for this church in comparison to other churches.

For example, he's clearly peeved at the Corinthians, and it feels like steam is coming out of Paul's ears when he writes to the Galatians, whereas Philippians is one of his warmest letters. But even though the Philippians' love and charity gave Paul confidence that they would persevere, it didn't give him false assurance. He still prayed that their "love may abound" so they "may be pure and blameless for the day of Christ" (Phil. 1:9-10). In chapter three of the letter, Paul worries about the circumcision party and other apostates within the community. One Protestant scholar concludes, "Paul does not seem to suggest that every individual Philippian believer will necessarily persevere to final salvation."[90]

The good works we do are only because God, through his grace, is working through us. But this grace is not irresistible. We are still free to say no to God. God works in us, but we also work by allowing God to do this. That's why Paul calls us God's "co-workers" in 1 Cor. 3:9.

Indeed, Paul cautions each of the Philippians to "work out your own salvation with fear and trembling" (Phil. 2:12). This doesn't mean that Christians must do a certain number of good works in order to be saved. It means that we have a responsibility to remain united to Christ because we are free to reject him. But we know that we don't hang on to Christ through our *own* power because, as the next verse says, "God is at work in you, both to will and to work for his good pleasure."

What Is Predestination?

Predestination is a complicated theological topic, which isn't surprising given that it focuses on how a timeless, eternal God knows and plans the future but in the process doesn't turn us into puppets by taking away our free will. It's a topic that would take its own book (or frankly several books) to properly address. Since this book is about what we must *do* to be saved, we won't be diving into this deep end of the systematic theology pool.

However, we do need to understand that God's predestination is real and at the same time that it does not preclude our responsibility to freely choose to accept rather than reject God's offer of salvation. The *Catechism* puts it this way: "To God, all moments of time are present in their immediacy. When therefore he establishes his eternal plan of 'predestination,' he includes in it each person's free response to his grace" (600).

God isn't ignorant of the future, just sitting up in heaven hoping everything will work out. God sees the past, present, and future in one glorious eternal moment. It's sort of like how you and I (if we were far smarter than we are now) could "see" an entire novel laid out in front of us if we took every page out of the book and arranged them in a grid. In *Mere Christianity*, C.S. Lewis notes how the author of a fictional story could be "timeless" from the characters' perspectives, by seeing the whole story at once in his mind before he writes it, and yet still enter into the story at particular points and interact with the characters (just as God sees all of time but could still become man).

But as I said, God also isn't a puppet master who maneuvers his creatures to do whatever he has already planned. God is so smart, which makes sense given his omniscience, that he can have a glorious plan for the entire universe that takes into account what he knows each of us will freely do in any given situation.

Some Christians say that when God predestines Christians to salvation that means we can never lose our salvation. God planned it, that settles it. But this forgets that God can predestine (or "foreknow") that we will initially choose to accept his grace and become Christian but not persevere in that choice. Those Christians are like the seeds in Jesus' parable that fall on shallow soil. They spring up at first but then wither in the sun and perish (Matt. 13:5-6).

In Ephesians 1:4, Paul says that God "chose us in him before the foundation of the world, that we should be holy and blameless before him." That's true: Christ will bring the Church to salvation. But whether *we* remain in a saving union with the Church depends on our cooperation with God's grace given to us on earth. Paul makes this clear in Colossians 1:22–23, where he says that Christ's crucifixion allows him to present us "holy and blameless and irreproachable before him, *provided that you continue in the Faith* [emphasis added], stable and steadfast, not shifting from the hope of the gospel which you heard."

Our salvation involves not just our union with Christ, but our union with the Church he established. When Christ brings his Church, his mystical body, into heaven, will we be within it or outside it?

OBJECTION 9:

Faith Alone, Apart from Works

"Catholicism contradicts the gospel because the Bible clearly teaches a man is justified by faith and not the works of the law. We do not have to work for our salvation. All we must do is receive it by faith alone."

"Being just simply means being with Christ and in Christ. And this suffices. Further observances are no longer necessary. For this reason, Luther's phrase 'faith alone' is true."

Who said this?

You might think it was a popular Protestant pastor or theologian. But it's actually from a Wednesday morning audience given by Pope Benedict XVI.[91] And he's not the only Catholic who has said we are saved or justified by "faith alone." Hilary of Poitiers said in the fourth century, "This was forgiven by Christ through faith, because the law could not yield, for faith alone justifies."[92]

What gives? Were Martin Luther and the other Protestant Reformers right all along?

As I said before, this book is about what one must do to be saved, so we will not be diving into the long and complicated history of the doctrine of *justification*, or what makes us right before God. However, some Protestants claim that because we are justified by *faith alone*, the only thing that can affect our relationship with God is faith and not anything we do.

But this reasoning fails, because it misunderstands the nature of "faith."

"Faith Alone" Is True, If . . .

Let me share a bit more from Pope Benedict XVI. Luther's phrase "faith alone" is true if it is not opposed to faith in charity, in love. Faith is looking at Christ, entrusting oneself to Christ, being united to Christ, conformed to Christ, to his life.

In many of St. Paul's letters he is combatting the heretical idea that in order to be a good Christian you must first be a good Jew. When Christianity spread only among Jews, this wasn't a problem. But when the gospel reached the Gentiles, some people, called *Judaizers*, claimed that in order to enter the New Covenant one first had to be a part of the Old Covenant. And this included being circumcised (you can see how that would be off-putting to potential male converts!). That's why Paul says in Romans 3:28 that "a man is justified by faith apart from works of law."

To be saved, you just need to be united to Christ, and circumcision is not necessary for that.

Some people think that Paul was actually combatting the false idea that a person has to do certain good works in order to get into heaven and that he was teaching "salvation by grace" instead. But the Jews of Paul's time *already* believed they were saved by grace. After all, God had chosen for them to be born among the chosen people, and no one thinks that having the right parents is a "good work." That's one thing we all know is outside our control. The Jews believed that salvation involved a public affirmation of God's gracious work, not unlike how some Protestants say that baptism shows the world we are saved but isn't itself what saves us.

Paul's response was that salvation comes, not from belonging to a certain group of people, but from belonging to *Christ*, which is something that *anyone*, regardless of birth, can possess by faith. That's why, immediately after Romans 3:28, Paul says, "Or is God the God of Jews only? Is he not the God of Gentiles also?" It's also why Paul says in Galatians 5:6, "For in Christ Jesus neither circumcision nor uncircumcision is of any avail, but faith working through love."

We see the same concern in Ephesians 2:8–9. Paul says we are saved by grace through faith and not because of works, lest anyone should boast. Indeed, the first moment of our salvation is a gift we receive, not a wage we work toward. But in the next verse Paul says, "For we are his workmanship, created in Christ Jesus for good works, which God prepared beforehand, that we should walk in them."

It seems clear that Paul has in mind two things: "works" that do not save and "good works" that God wants us to perform. The works that Paul is condemning are those that give someone the Jewish identity that he thinks he needs in order to be saved—not good deeds done to please God. This is clear in verse 11: "Therefore remember that at one time you Gentiles in the flesh, called the uncircumcision by what is called the circumcision, which is made in the flesh by hands." Even non-Christian scholars like Bart Ehrman admit that

> when Paul speaks of "works" he is explicitly referring to "works of the law," that is, observance of Jewish rules governing circumcision, the Sabbath, kosher foods, and the like. When James speaks of works, he means something like "good deeds." Paul himself would not argue that a person could have faith without doing good deeds.[93]

As I previously noted, the Bible discusses how salvation awaits those who believe in Christ *to the end*. Romans 10:9 says, "If you confess with your lips that Jesus is Lord and believe in your heart that God raised him from the dead, you will be saved." This doesn't mean that salvation is for anyone who *ever* confessed "Jesus is Lord" because, as we've seen, Christ said there would be many who cried "Lord, Lord" at one time but *not* enter the kingdom (Matt. 7:21). Salvation is for those who presently believe and confess Christ in word and deed.

This isn't about performing certain good deeds, or a certain number of good deeds, in order to be saved. Paul is saying that we are saved by grace and damned by choice. In Romans 11:22, he even warns Gentile Christians who feel superior because so many Jews rejected Jesus as the Messiah, telling them not to gloat: "Note then the kindness and the severity of God: severity toward those who have fallen, but God's kindness to you, provided you continue in his kindness; otherwise *you too will be cut off*" (emphasis added).

Faith Alone or *Faithfulness* Alone?

It's important to note that the Judaizer heresy was about more than just circumcision, though that was a big part of it. The phrase "works of law," the thing by which Paul says a man is not justified, also included the moral precepts of the Old Covenant, including the moral code found in the Ten Commandments (it can also be translated, "Works of Torah").[94]

Here, Paul was condemning those who obeyed laws like the Ten Commandments simply because they were what made a person a good Jew. Paul allowed people to retain Jewish customs like feast days (Rom. 14:5), provided they did not impose these practices on others (Rom. 14:10) or trust in those practices for their salvation (Gal. 3:10).

Protestants err when they think that because Paul condemned people for requiring something God never imposed (such as circumcision) this means God *only* requires faith for salvation. Paul's curse upon the Judaizers shows that true Christians can lose their salvation if they disobey God by seeking salvation in another covenant. That's why Paul told those Christians who tried to receive salvation through circumcision, "You are severed from Christ, you who would be justified by the law; you have fallen away from grace" (Gal. 5:4).

Just because keeping the Old Covenant is not necessary for salvation, it doesn't follow that every law *in* the Old Covenant is no longer necessary for salvation. Jimmy Akin provides a good example: just because drinking Diet Coke isn't necessary for good health (and may even detract from it), that doesn't mean that *water,* which is the principal ingredient in Diet Coke, is not necessary for good health.[95] As I note in my book *The Case for Catholicism*:

> Saying someone is justified by faith apart from works of the law is not the same as saying he is justified by faith alone. If I say, "A man is made healthy by medicine apart from quack cures," that is not the same as saying, "A man is made healthy by medicine alone apart from quack cures." Medicine divorced from exercise and healthy diet cannot make someone healthy, just as faith divorced from charity and obedience cannot make someone justified.[96]

We are saved by "faith alone" if we understand "faith" as something more like *faithfulness*: an act of the will that keeps a person united to Christ. St. Augustine said in the fifth century, "We should advise the faithful that they would endanger the salvation of their souls if they acted on the false assurance that faith alone is sufficient for salvation or that they need not perform good works in order to be saved."[97] This was why Martin Luther said of Augustine, "When the door was opened for me in Paul, so that I understood what justification by faith is, it was all over with Augustine."[98]

For Augustine, as well as for the Catholic Church today, faith isn't just believing the right things—since even the demons believe that one God exists and they tremble in his presence (James 2:19). Instead, a person is saved if he is united to Christ and remains faithful to him until death. In remaining faithful to God, we are not "following rules in order to earn salvation." We are, instead, cooperating with God's grace and feely choosing not to reject him in word or deed. As Augustine put it in a way that echoes Galatians 5:6, "It can be said that God's commandments pertain to *faith alone*, if it is not dead [faith], but rather understood as that live faith, which works through love."[99] This is a theme that is continued in the letter of James, which we will examine next.

OBJECTION 10:

Saving Faith Is Never Alone

"When the Bible says we are not justified by 'faith alone,' it is talking about a *dead faith* that we know is dead because it has no works. We are saved by a *living faith*, which can always be identified because it produces good works."

When I ask Protestants about their belief that works are just "fruits" or "signs" of already-accomplished salvation, I often find that what they actually believe isn't far off from what Catholics believe. At first, they say that a true Christian will have visible good works in their life, like feeding the homeless. But what if a Christian does other good works instead, like visiting the elderly? They then backtrack, like that woman I mentioned in chapter 2, and say, "Well, there's no *specific* good works. There will just be good works of some kind."

I then ask them questions that highlight the anxiety this can produce. Can I know I am truly saved if I don't publicly go out every month, or every week, or even every day and do some kind of good work for my neighbor? Or maybe I could do many good works the first year I am a Christian, and then take a break for a few years before starting up again?

At this point they backtrack even further and say that the good works will vary in kind and frequency, but what's constant in a true Christian is the absence of behaviors incompatible with the Christian life (i.e. mortal sins).

And as a Catholic I would agree. The only good work that "saves us" is the good work of remaining in Christ by not rejecting him through unrepented grave evil. This rejection can take the form of committing gravely evil acts (commission) or failing to do the good we ought to do (omission).

I understand why Catholics would cite where James says, "You see that a man is justified by works and not by faith alone" (2:24). But if we're not careful, this can lead people to think that Catholics believe themselves to be *initially justified* through some good work. As we've seen, this is completely false. The *Catechism* says that "no one can merit the initial grace of forgiveness and justification, at the beginning of conversion" (2010). The Council of Trent said that nothing we do, neither faith nor works, initially justifies us. Salvation is a gift we simply receive from God, who always moves first within us. The council cites James 2:24 only to refer to good works done *after* we are saved, not works that are done *to be* saved.

But why do these works matter at all?

Once you accept that Christians can forsake their salvation, you're better able to see, as I noted in chapter nine, that we are in a spiritual war. It's not like salvation and damnation just exist as abstract rewards or punishments we stumble upon. Good works increase our holiness and spiritually strengthen us to do good and avoid evil. Good works don't get us to heaven, but they keep us out of hell by drawing us near to God and away from the Evil One and his temptations.

The Light of Christ

Catholics and Protestants agree that James is not talking about becoming right in God's eyes by doing good works. No work can do that. At the beginning of our salvation, when we first receive Christ, we receive the light of his righteousness infused into our souls. We cannot increase the *quality* of this righteousness because it comes from God alone, but we can increase it in *quantity* of expression.

This is what it means to cooperate with God's grace to "grow" in holiness. We do this by performing the good works he prepared beforehand for us to do, as Paul says in Ephesians 2:10. That's why the *Catechism* says "Grace, by uniting us to Christ in active love, ensures the supernatural quality of our acts and consequently their merit before God and before men. The saints have always had a lively awareness that their merits were pure grace" (2011). Jimmy Akin compares the quality and quantity of our justification to the purity and brightness of the light of a lamp:

> Even if a light is pure white, it may be either dim or bright. One could thus take a lamp that is emitting pure white light and turn up the intensity so that it shines more brightly. In the same way, after God has given a person a pure righteousness before him, he may by his grace lead that person to grow in the quantity of righteousness he has.[100]

This parallels Jesus' command to "let your light so shine before men, that they may see your good works and give glory to your Father who is in heaven" (Matt. 5:16). We can't change the quality of Christ's pure righteousness given to us in baptism, but we can cooperate with God and choose whether this righteousness we exhibit in our works will be as dim as a single candle or as bright as a spotlight that clearly reveals Christ to the world.

But Protestants who deny that our righteousness can increase often claim that James is not saying good works affect our justification. He is just saying that good works simply show we have "true, living faith" rather than "false, dead faith." To prove this, they usually cite James 2:14: "What does it profit, my brethren, if a man says he has faith but has not works? Can his faith save him?"

They claim that the person in James's example only "says" he has faith. He doesn't *really* have faith because he doesn't have the good works that accompany faith. The paraphrase of this passage in the extremely loose Bible translation known as *The Message* summarizes what many Protestants think James is saying: "Does merely talking about faith indicate that a person really has it?"

But in the original Greek text of the passage, James doesn't say, "Can *his* faith save him," which might be interpreted as pointing to this man's own deficient, dead kind of faith. Instead, the verse just says, "Can *the faith* save him?" or "Can *faith* save him?" Likewise, when James says, "Faith by itself, if it has no works, is dead," he is not contrasting real faith with a different thing called "dead faith." James never talks about a thing called "dead faith." There is only faith, and it is always a good thing.

James 2:26 says, "For as the body apart from the spirit is dead, so faith apart from works is dead." What makes faith "alive" is not belief or even trust in God—it's works! Just as the spirit is distinct from the body and is what gives it life, works are distinct from faith and they are what make that faith—the one kind of faith there is—alive and salvific.

So, James is not telling people to have the *kind* of faith that always produces good works. His message is for those with faith to complete and enliven their faith by choosing to do good works. He is telling them to do good works that make their faith grow and thrive, and especially not to perform evil works that kill this faith. Doing good works and avoiding gravely evil works are not, as some Protestants allege, simply the automatic consequence of an authentic, saving faith. They are part of what makes that faith alive and saving. That's why Paul says in Romans 2:13, "For it is not the hearers of the law who are righteous before God, but the doers of the law who will be justified."

Justification Before God . . . or Men?

Other Protestants claim that James is only talking about being justified *before men*—that is, in the sight of other people. But consider James 2:21-22: "Was not Abraham our father justified by works, when he offered his son Isaac upon the altar? You see that faith was active along with his works, and faith was completed by works."

The problem with saying that this passage only refers to Abraham showing the good works of his authentic faith to other people is that Genesis 22:5 says that Abraham and Isaac were *by themselves* when Abraham offered Isaac to God. God was the only witness of this act, so the justification must be in *his* sight. The Protestant biblical scholar Thomas Schreiner affirms, "There is no evidence that justification here relates to justification before people rather than God. When James uses the words 'save' and 'justify,' he has in mind one's relationship with God."[101]

But remember, James is talking about a saved person growing in God's righteousness by cooperating with God to do good works. As Akin puts it, "This is the understanding the Catholic Church has of ongoing justification." Akin then cites the Council of Trent, which says that people who are initially justified "increase in that justice received through the grace of Christ and are further justified, as it is written: . . . 'Do you see that by works a man is justified, and not by faith only?'" (Jas. 2:24).[102]

The first moment we receive justification, or the "light of Christ," is when we are baptized. This is why part of the baptismal liturgy includes lighting a baptismal candle, and the celebrant says, "Parents and godparents, this light is entrusted to you to be kept burning brightly. This child of yours has been enlightened by Christ. He (she) is to walk always as a child of the light. May he (she) keep the flame of faith alive in his (her) heart."

But some Protestants say that our righteousness received from God cannot increase. Nothing we do can change what God sees in us because the only thing he sees is *Christ's* righteousness covering our sins and unworthiness. It is to that important claim we turn next.

OBJECTION 11:

Christ's Righteousness, Not Mine

"Salvation doesn't come from what we do. Salvation comes from having the perfect righteousness of Jesus Christ."

The late Protestant pastor John Macarthur considered one Bible verse to be the "heart of the gospel." It's not John 3:16: "For God so loved the world that he gave his only Son, that whoever believes in him should not perish but have eternal life." No, it's 2 Corinthians 5:20–21: "We beseech you on behalf of Christ, be reconciled to God. For our sake he made him to be sin who knew no sin, so that in him we might become the righteousness of God."

You might say this has little to do with the traditional view of the gospel being the hope we have in the life, death, and resurrection of Jesus Christ (1 Cor. 15). But some Protestants, in line with Macarthur, say that our salvation is found in our sins being legally transferred (or *imputed*) to Christ and then his righteousness being legally transferred to us. Through an act of faith, God "swaps" our sins for Christ's righteousness and that is why we can spend eternity with God.

Jesus doesn't literally become a sinner, but he is literally punished for our sins because now he has *become* our sins. Frances Turretin, a second-generation Protestant Reformer, said of Christ on the cross that "the sense of the divine wrath and vengeance [was] resting upon him."[103]

And in the other direction, God covers our sins with Christ's perfect righteousness. When God looks at us at the final judgment, he sees only Christ's righteousness. Martin Luther is believed to have compared this process of justification to how dung heaps in the countryside would be covered with pure white snow. The dung heap remains, but it's just no longer visible.

Therefore, some Protestants say, what we do after initial salvation does not affect our heavenly end, because God's judgment isn't based on *our* righteousness. It is only based on the perfect righteousness of Christ that covers our souls.

But this doesn't make sense from either a logical or a biblical perspective.

Once Saved, Always Saved?

Many Protestants say that if someone who allegedly took part in this "great exchange" but later became an apostate must have never received Christ's righteousness in the first place. They had a counterfeit conversion. But a fair number of other Protestants believe that a true Christian could go on to commit all kinds of grave sins, or even leave the Faith entirely, and still be saved, because his righteousness has nothing to do with his salvation.

These Protestants believe in "free grace theology" and they criticize other Protestants for being "closet Catholics." Catholics, they say, worry about not committing sin so that they don't lose their salvation in the future. But they claim that Protestants who worry about sin don't want to lose their salvation in the *past*—that is, discover they were "never saved in the first place."

They say this is just as stressful, and that it rejects the perfect righteousness of Christ we receive when we were saved—a righteousness that covers *every* sin we commit. This even includes the sin of permanently abandoning Christ. Free grace theologian Robert Wilkin says, "There is no time requirement on saving faith. Even if a person believes only for a while, he still has eternal life."[104]

Free grace theologians try to say that believers who sin will face a loss of *rewards* in heaven as a kind of punishment (which sounds like purgatory, which we'll discuss later). But how does that make sense if the only thing God sees in a sinner is Christ's perfect righteousness? Most Protestants believe that Christians will receive different rewards based on how they lived in this life. As St. Paul said, "He who plants and he who waters are equal, and each shall receive his wages according to his labor" (1 Cor. 3:8).

But if God only sees the same perfect righteousness of Christ in each of us, then God would have to treat each of us the exact the same way. But, since we know that God doesn't treat people in heaven as exact equals, due to the different rewards we will receive, that means God sees something *different* in each one of us. He sees the state of our own souls. Thus, if we are made fit to enter heaven, he will reward us differently based on how we conformed ourselves to him in this life.

Whipping Boy or Sacrificial Son?

Writings from late medieval Europe contain stories of young princes whose courts included other boys who would receive corporal punishment on their behalf, called "whipping boys." Under the view of salvation, defended by people like Macarthur, Christ becomes a kind of "whipping boy" who is punished on our behalf because he has "become" our sins. When the Father sees the Son on the cross, he sees our sins, and so pours out his wrath upon the Son.

But the Catholic Church teaches that "Jesus did not experience reprobation [punishment] as if he himself had sinned" (CCC 603). The Church also teaches that salvation is more than just a declaration of innocence; it is a transformation that makes us morally pure. The *Catechism* adds, citing the Council of Trent, "Moved by grace, man turns toward God and away from sin, thus accepting forgiveness and righteousness from on high. 'Justification is not only the remission of sins, but also the sanctification and renewal of the interior man'" (1989).

We know the verse, "he made him to be sin who knew no sin, so that in him we might become the righteousness of God" can't be *literally* true. Christ is sinless (Heb. 4:15), so he can't "become" our sins. And "the righteousness of God" is an abstract concept used to describe the infinite perfection of God. We don't "become" abstract concepts when we have faith in Christ. When we look to the history of the Church, and even the early Protestant Reformation, we see other more plausible interpretations of this verse.

Several early Christians said this was an allusion to Christ coming in the likeness of sinful flesh, or just the Incarnation in general, and has nothing to do with imputation of sin. St. Augustine said, "Therefore having no sin of his own; nevertheless, on account of the likeness of sinful flesh in which he came, he was called sin, that he might be sacrificed to wash away sin."[105] Even John Calvin used this verse in this way.[106]

The point is not that Christ had to "become our sins" so we could be saved. It was that Christ was able to offer himself for humanity by taking human nature and a human body. This corresponds to Romans 8:3, which says, "For God has done what the law, weakened by the flesh, could not do: sending his own Son in the likeness of sinful flesh and for sin, he condemned sin in the flesh."

A Transformative "Sin Offering"

Another interpretation of 2 Corinthians 5:21 is that "made him to be sin" means "made him to be a sin offering." The Greek word for sin in this passage can also mean "sin offering" or that which is sacrificed to take away sin. Hebrews 10:6 is quoting Psalm 40, which refers to sacrifices. It literally says in Greek, "Burnt offerings and for sin you have not delighted in," so most translators render "sin" in this passage as "sin offering" because that makes the most sense of the context.

It's reasonable to conclude the same is true of 2 Corinthians 5:21, because Paul makes it clear that Christ himself is a paschal sacrifice. He says in 1 Corinthians 5:7, "Cleanse out the old leaven that you may be a new lump, as you really are unleavened. For Christ, our paschal lamb, has been sacrificed." And John the Baptist calls Jesus "the Lamb of God, who takes away the sin of the world" (John 1:29).

This verse is compatible with the Catholic view of Christ's death: not being an occasion for the Father to punish the Son but the time when the Son offered himself as a perfect sacrifice that pays the debt to God incurred by every sin ever committed. It is then up to each person to allow God to apply the effects of Christ's sacrifice to his or her soul by repenting, receiving, and remaining in Christ. As we noted earlier, it's why Hebrews 10:26–27 says, "For if we sin deliberately after receiving the knowledge of the truth, there no longer remains a sacrifice for sins, but a fearful prospect of judgment."

Instead, we should take heart that Christ doesn't just legally expunge our sinful deeds from a ledger. He *transforms* us as we receive his righteousness. 2 Corinthians 5:17 says, "Therefore, if any one is in Christ, he is a new creation; the old has passed away, behold, the new has come."

Some of my Protestant friends say that a Christian cannot lose his status as a child of God just as my children will never stop being my children. It's true that my children will never cease having their genetic relationship with me, but they *can* abandon me (look up "Adult-Child Estrangement" to see some sad examples of this). Likewise, baptism leaves an indelible mark on our soul, which is why it is never repeated, even if we completely leave the Faith and then return.

When God looks at me or any other baptized person, he does not only see the righteousness of his son. He sees one of his beloved children infused with the righteousness of Christ. My good works genuinely please God because, through baptism, he becomes my Father and he sees me as a son pleasing him through obedience rather than a rebel trying to appease him with worthless human deeds. And even though my sins can distance me from God or even turn me into a prodigal son, nothing can undo the filial relationship created in baptism, which is why we can return to God as prodigal sons and he is always willing to forgive our sons and heal our broken souls.

OBJECTION 12:

Purgatory Makes Christ's Death Insufficient

"Catholics don't believe salvation is by grace alone because they think you still have to suffer for your sins in purgatory—even though Christ paid for *all* of our sins."

Once I watched an anti-Catholic documentary, and this line about the souls in purgatory stopped me cold: "If they have enough people praying for them, and if they do enough time in purgatory, they might possibly get to heaven."

I threw up my hands and shouted at the TV: "No!"

I wish those involved in the film had simply searched for the word *purgatory* in the *Catechism* because, if they had, they would have seen this is 100 percent false. Purgatory is for those who *are* saved, not those trying to be saved. And they would've known it if they'd read this:

> All who die in God's grace and friendship, but still imperfectly purified, are indeed assured of their eternal salvation; but after death they undergo purification, so as to achieve the holiness necessary to enter the joy of heaven. The Church gives the name purgatory to this final purification of the elect, which is entirely different from the punishment of the damned" (CCC 1031-1032).

Purgatory is not an alternative to heaven or hell, and it is not a "second chance" to be saved. It is not a place where sinners work to purify themselves in order "to get out quickly." It is a place of sanctification for those on their way to heaven.

Protestants already believe in sanctification so they should have no problem accepting this final part of that process. Indeed, the Protestant author C.S. Lewis compared purgatory to visiting a dentist, and even observed, "Our souls demand purgatory, don't they?"[107]

We can know that this process (and it is a process; the Church doesn't teach that purgatory is a "place") happens to some Christians via a simple logical argument.

The Argument from Purification

1. God can purify saved Christians of their desire for sin.
2. No one in heaven will desire sin.
3. Some saved Christians still desire sin at the moment of their death.
4. Therefore, some Christians will be purified of the desire for sin after death but before they enter heaven.

Premise one follows from Scripture and God's omnipotence: if God can't free us from the desire to sin, then he isn't all-powerful. Premise two follows from Revelation 21:27, which says of heaven that "nothing unclean shall enter it." In heaven there will be no actual sin or even the desire to sin. And premise three is known from experience, especially in cases of Christians who die unexpectedly while they are struggling with venial sins.

To get around this argument, some people cite Hebrews 10:14: "For by a single offering he has perfected for all time those who are sanctified." However, Paul says in Philippians 3:12 that he is not yet perfect, and in Romans 7:20 he says that he does evil because of "sin which dwells within me." But neither Paul, nor any other Christian, can deal with this indwelling sin in heaven. They need to be purified first, and the Church gives the name "purgatory" to this process.

Some people claim that this purification happens the moment our souls leave our bodies, since we are no longer tempted to do evil by our fleshy bodies. But we know that the souls of the *damned* aren't freed from sin when they leave their body to go to hell. This means something else must happen to the souls of the saved, the *elect*, who are attached to sin in this life but cannot have this attachment to sin in the next life. This "something else" is the process of purgatory. And, just as we cooperate with our sanctification in this life, it stands to reason that we will cooperate with sanctification after death, but not in a way by which we "earn" our holiness.

Some Protestants will counter that all Christians go to heaven immediately after death, because in Philippians 1:23 Paul describes his desire to die and be with Christ and in 2 Corinthians 5:8-9 he (allegedly) says "to be absent from the body is to be at home with the Lord."

But many Catholics today talk about dying and going to heaven without mentioning purgatory. This doesn't mean they don't believe in it. You or I might say that we desire to leave the office and be at home with our family, but that doesn't mean we won't have a commute or some other interim period that exists between leaving the office and arriving home. I certainly *want* to be at home with the Lord, and this is expressed in the *correct* quotation of 2 Corinthians 5:8-9, which says that "we would *rather* be away from the body and at home with the Lord"—not the common misquote "to be absent from the body is to be present with the Lord," or still less "immediately present" with the Lord.

Just one verse later, Paul reveals that after death we don't immediately enter into heaven free from any purification or even punishment. Instead, he says that "we must all appear before the judgment seat of Christ, so that each one may receive good or evil, according to what he has done in the body" (2 Cor. 5:10). Paul even says that some Christians who acted against God's will would still be saved, but only as "through fire" (1 Cor. 3:15), suggesting some kind of difficult trial between death and heaven.

According to the third-century Christian author Tertullian, "No one, on becoming absent from the body, is at once a dweller in the presence of the Lord, except by the prerogative of martyrdom."[108] Whereas a martyr's reward was immediate entrance into heaven, the early Church recognized that other believers would have to be purified of sinful desires after death before entering into heavenly bliss. This is why St. Augustine wrote, in his *City of God*, "Of those who suffer temporary punishments after death, all are not doomed to those everlasting pains which are to follow that judgment." He also speaks of some who will "not only be saved from eternal punishments, but shall not even suffer purgatorial torments after death."[109]

The Argument from Punishment

Many Protestants misconstrue purgatory as a place of *transaction*, in which sinners must suffer in order to "pay God" for the offenses they've committed against him. Upon receiving payment, God raises the heavenly tollbooth gate, so to speak, and the sinner is now free to walk into heaven. But Catholics instead view purgatory as the final stage of the sanctifying moral correction God already gives us *in this life*—a training that purifies us from sin and prepares us for heaven.

As we saw in previous chapters, Christ atoned not just for our sins but for the sins of the entire world (1 John 2:2). But that doesn't mean that everyone in the world is going to heaven. Each of us must choose whether we will cooperate with God and allow him to apply to our souls the saving grace Christ merited on the cross. The sacrifice Christ made, and only that sacrifice, is capable of atoning or making up for the eternal consequences of our sins. But our sins also have non-eternal consequences that are called *temporal punishments*. The *Catechism* explains the temporal consequences of sin this way:

> Every sin, even venial, entails an unhealthy attachment to creatures, which must be purified either here on earth, or after death in the state called purgatory. This purification frees one from what is called the "temporal punishment" of sin. These two punishments must not be conceived of as a kind of vengeance inflicted by God from without, but as following from the very nature of sin (1472).

When I punish my children, I don't do it because I like watching them suffer or because I think they "owe me" a certain amount of suffering in order to be free and happy. Punishment helps their wills become *realigned to the good*, so that they will more naturally make a good choice when the temptation to do evil rears its ugly head again. And God does the same thing for Christians—both before and after death. These temporary punishments realign our wills so that we are better prepared to choose to remain in Christ and receive eternal bliss. Consider this argument:

1. When Christians sin, God unpleasantly disciplines them to morally perfect them.

2. Some sins are not unpleasantly disciplined in this life.
3. Therefore, God unpleasantly disciplines some Christians after death to morally perfect them.

The first premise is well attested in Scripture. When King David committed adultery and murder and then repented, God forgave him, so he did not lose his salvation. However, God did allow David to suffer in this life because of his sins by allowing his firstborn son to die. Why would God do that? Well, the question, "Why does God let us suffer because we've sinned?" is part of the larger question "Why does God let us suffer at all?" This mystery is known as the *problem of evil*, and although we don't have every answer to this question, we do know that God, who is unlimited in power and goodness, can always bring more good from any evil he allows to occur.

When it comes to suffering in response to sin, or punishment, that good reason may be moral correction. Scripture notes that

> we have had earthly fathers to discipline us and we respected them. Shall we not much more be subject to the Father of spirits and live? For they disciplined us for a short time at their pleasure, but he disciplines us for our good, that we may share his holiness. For the moment all discipline seems painful rather than pleasant; later it yields the peaceful fruit of righteousness to those who have been trained by it (Heb. 12:9-11).

The author of Hebrews says that our fathers disciplined us "at their pleasure," which means that sometimes the punishment wasn't justified. I remember, as a kid, when an eight-year-old neighbor said absolutely mean things to me about how I looked, and then he told his mom that *I* said those things to him—leading to a painful (and unjust) punishment from my parents. But God would never do that to us. When God disciplines us, it is perfectly just and only "for our good, that we may share his holiness." This shows that even though those who are in Christ have no (eternal) condemnation (Rom. 8:1), it doesn't follow that they won't experience a father's loving discipline through corrective punishment.

Saved Through Fire

With regard to premise two: in 1 Corinthians 3:10-15, Paul describes Christian workers at the final judgment. Those who produced good works in life are symbolized by precious stones. Those who produced bad works are symbolized by hay and straw. A fire tests the works and burns up the bad ones. Verse fifteen says: "If any man's work is burned up, he will suffer loss, though he himself will be saved, but only as through fire."

The Greek word translated word as "suffer loss" in 1 Corinthians 3:15 (*zemiothesetai*) refers to "punishment" in this passage. The Protestant scholar E.P. Sanders says of this chapter of 1 Corinthians, "Paul is discussing people who will be saved, but they will be commended or *lightly punished* at the judgment, depending on their deeds" (emphasis added).[110]

Some Protestants say this passage has nothing to do with punishment for sin but only refers to Christians with bad motivations who will suffer the "loss" of rewards. But that *is* a punishment for sin! When my own children misbehave, I often punish them by withholding a reward they otherwise would have received.

Even though Christ saves us from the eternal consequences of our sins, God still allows us to suffer the *temporary consequences* of our sins. These include having a disordered will that is attached to sin, a lack of full fellowship with God because of this disordered will, and even suffering in this life from our sins. And if God unpleasantly disciplines us (as the author of Hebrews would put it) in this life for our moral good, why wouldn't God do that after death?

Finally, purgatory doesn't detract from the work of Christ because it simply *is* the work of Christ. As Pope Benedict XVI put it, "Some recent theologians are of the opinion that the fire which both burns and saves is Christ himself, the Judge and Savior. The encounter with him is the decisive act of judgment. Before his gaze all falsehood melts away" (*Spe Salvi* 47).

OBJECTION 13:

Catholics Think They Can Buy Tickets to Heaven

"The Catholic Church has no understanding of the gospel of Jesus Christ. For example, it still offers 'indulgences,' which allow you to pay for your sins and buy salvation!"

There are many misconceptions about indulgences. These include the claim that indulgences are passes into heaven that were sold during the Middle Ages, allowing someone to "indulge" in sin and still be saved. Even some Catholics think indulgences only exist to help us "stay out of purgatory." But to truly understand indulgences we need to have a proper framework for understanding God's judgment of sin.

As we've seen, purgatory is not a place we need to avoid visiting, like a tourist trap on the highway. Staying out of purgatory is simply a matter of avoiding the one thing purgatory purifies us of—sin. That's simple, but not easy. Our fallen human nature leaves us subject to *concupiscence*: the internal inclination to sin that we must constantly battle against. That's why the Church urges us to "strive by works of mercy and charity, as well as by prayer and the various practices of penance, to put off completely the 'old man' and to put on the 'new man'" (CCC 1473).

As we grow in holiness, we sin less and less, but almost all of us still inevitably sin. Through the sacrament of reconciliation, we are restored to the communion with God that mortal sin made us lose; but all sins, mortal and venial, still leave a temporary effect on our souls. They persist in the form of attachments to sin that are not removed by the sacrament of confession alone. Is there a way to purge the effects of sin from our souls before death and thus remove the need to for purification after death?

Yes. The Church teaches that the temporary punishment for sin can be remitted, which forms the basis for the practice of granting an indulgence.

Tickets to Heaven?

In this book, we are mostly talking about what we need to get to heaven. But we don't *need* a single indulgence. Indulgences cannot forgive a single sin; they do not provide a "get out of hell free card" as appears in some caricatures of this Catholic practice.

But for many Christians, indulgences can be an aid to the sanctification without which none of us can go to heaven. For although Christ's sacrificial death takes away the eternal punishment of sin (hell), we've seen that temporary consequences or punishments can remain. For this reason, God corrects us in order to realign our will toward him as the highest good.

Now, God doesn't *have* to do it this way. He *could* will for us to be made perfectly holy in an instant—in the same way that he didn't *have* to create us in a fallen state in the first place or didn't *have* to die on the cross to save us. But it was *fitting* that he do both those things, and it is fitting that he create human beings who, through his grace merited on the cross, conquer sin and the effects of the fall, and that he allow those human beings to undergo moral correction thereafter in order to remove any attachment to sin they have.

The fact that we desire to "make up" for our sins shows that suffering temporary consequences of sin coheres with our human nature. It dignifies our status as creatures who cooperate with God's will for our lives. It doesn't take away from the purely gracious nature of God's saving work, a work we do not earn but merely accept with eternal gratitude. And since these temporary punishments (or "temporal punishments," as they are more often called, because they happen in this time of life) are not necessary for our sanctification, the Church can ask God to remove them. According to the *Catechism*, "An indulgence is partial or plenary according as it removes either part or all of the temporal punishment due to sin" (CCC 1471).

A partial indulgence, which removes some but not all of the temporal punishments associated with sin, can be obtained by performing with a contrite heart the work to which the indulgence is attached (a list of these works can be found in the "Enchiridion of Indulgences"). A plenary indulgence can be obtained by performing the work while also being in a state of grace, being completely detached from sin, going to confession, receiving the Eucharist, and praying for the intentions of the pope.

The Church does this to fulfill its mission to save souls, not for profit. The myth that indulgences were "sold" comes from the Middle Ages, when one of the good works that could be performed to remove some temporal punishment was the giving of alms to a charitable organization or to the Church. Giving away money that we'd rather spend on ourselves is a good thing that not only helps the needy but trains our wills stop loving things of the flesh and prefer things of the spirit—and so is a great example of the moral correction that prepares us for heaven.

Since "the love of money is the root of all evil" (1 Tim. 6:10), however, this practice of seeking indulgences through almsgiving became corrupt and transactional. People fell into the habit of merely giving away excess money without spiritual attachment, and some Church officials saw this money as a way to provide for the Church rather than as an expression of sorrow for sin. Because of this potential for abuse, the Church later prohibited almsgiving from being a good work associated with indulgences.

The *Catechism* also says that we can have all the temporary punishments for sin removed by an authentic rejection of sin and a corresponding embrace of God's love. "A conversion which proceeds from a fervent charity," it says, "can attain the complete purification of the sinner in such a way that no punishment would remain (1472). This is similar to how a person can be forgiven of sin by making a perfect act of contrition, expressing to God genuine sorrow for having offended him, even if he is unable to make a sacramental confession. In both cases, God mercifully heals sinners even beyond the ordinary means he has provided. This reveals a well-trodden path, aided by the ministers of the Church, to help people reach their blessed end.

A "Treasury of Merit"?

Many Protestants hear terms like "the treasury of merit" and about good works being applied to the souls in purgatory, and it sounds way too transactional, divorced from the simple message of Christ's sacrifice atoning for sin. But although such terms may be off-putting to Protestants, the concepts should be familiar to them.

For example: if by *merit* we mean "a trade of value for equal value," then neither good works nor the prayers of Mary and the saints "merit" anything. Only Christ can merit grace for us in that sense, because he trades his infinitely valuable life as the God-man for God's infinitely valuable favor, his grace.

But if by *merit* we mean "reward," then *any* Christian can merit grace from God. The Bible is full of references of the saints being "rewarded" (in Greek *misthos*, literally "a wage") for their good deeds. The reward is not a strict value-for-value accounting but a gratuitous arrangement proceeding from God's generous goodness.

When I pay my first-grader five dollars for raking leaves, it isn't because he performed five dollars' worth of work on the open market (his leafy pile isn't the most professional). Rather, my son obeyed my command out of filial love, and so he "merited" the money in virtue of my *promise* to him, not in virtue of the work he did. And God does something similar: he promises to reward his children for their good deeds and he does so because of that promise, not because of the strict value of the works his children perform.

Furthermore, Protestants can recognize that our good deeds can benefit other members of the body of Christ. For example, Paul said that the Jews of his time were "beloved for the sake of their forefathers" (Rom. 11:28). God had mercy on the city of Sodom because of Abraham's intercession. Paul even said that in his own flesh he "complete[s] what is lacking in Christ's afflictions for the sake of his body, that is, the church" (Col. 1:24).

Of course, the only thing "missing" in Christ's perfect sacrifice is *our sacrifice* that is united to his and makes it even more pleasing to God. Asking God to be merciful to Christians who are being sanctified after death doesn't take away from Christ's work, any more than asking God to be merciful to Christians being sanctified *before death* does. In both cases, the Church recognizes its humble duty to care for all parts of the body of Christ, including the parts that have died in God's friendship and await their heavenly reward.

In the second century, a bishop named Abercius asked that the simple request "Pray for Abercius" be put on his tombstone.[111] Tombs in ancient underground cemeteries, called *catacombs*, also contain requests for prayers for the person's soul and even requests that saints pray for the person after his death. One reads: "Peter and Paul, help Primus, a sinner."[112]

Around A.D. 375, St. Epiphanius wrote in answer to an objection to prayers for the dead in the liturgy. The heretic involved, Aerius, had asked, "Why do you mention the names of the dead after their deaths [in the liturgy]? If the living prays or has given alms, how will this benefit the dead?" Epiphanius replied,

> As to naming the dead, what could be more helpful? What could be more opportune or wonderful than that the living believe that the departed are alive and have not ceased to be but exist, and live with the Lord—and that the most sacred doctrine should declare that there is hope for those who pray for their brethren as though they were off on a journey? And even though the prayer we offer for them cannot root out all their faults—[how could it], since we often slip in this world, inadvertently and deliberately—it is still useful as an indication of something more perfect.[113]

OBJECTION 14:

What About Scandal?

"How can you say that the Catholic Church gives us salvation when it's so infested with bad leaders and scandalous acts?"

I was baptized and received into the Catholic Church in March of 2002, one of the worst periods in recent memory to tell people that you want to become Catholic! That's because just two months prior, reporters with the *Boston Globe* broke the story about how the Archdiocese of Boston had covered up allegations of priests sexually abusing children. The story became a catalyst that led to the revelation of similar problems in other dioceses in the United States and across the world.

One of my non-Catholic friends wryly told me before my baptism, "Nice job picking a new religion, Trent."

For many people, the claim that "salvation is from the Catholic Church" is incompatible with the reality of sin and scandal among its members, especially the clergy. In my book *Why We're Catholic* I devoted a whole chapter to this problem, arguing that to abandon God's Church because some of its leaders have sinned is as foolish as abandoning a hospital that has the medicine you need to live because its governing body is corrupt.

Or to put it another way: you don't leave Peter because of what Judas did.

Another group of people says that isn't just the sexual abuse scandal that causes them to question the Church's unique role in our salvation. For them, the Church's leaders cause scandal when they fail to suppress LGBT "Pride Masses" or name defenders of moral and theological error to advisory bodies in the Vatican.[114] How can salvation come from the Catholic Church when its leaders create so many scandalous stumbling blocks?

The Chosen People or Bust

The Nicene Creed says that God's Church is *one*, *holy*, *catholic*, and *apostolic*. So far, we've seen the importance of there being one Church, its being universal, and its having apostolic authority. But what do we mean when we say that Church is "holy"?

It would be a mistake to conclude that the mark of holiness requires the true Church to be perfectly faultless and saintly in all its members and leaders. Such a Church does not exist and never will exist.

Instead, by "holy" we mean that God's true Church, the Catholic Church, has been given by God the means to *make us holy*, to set us apart for God. And this remains true even if some of its leaders fail to use these means for themselves—just as it's true that a doctor can have the means to treat cancer even if he himself smokes cigarettes and eats processed foods.

And this has been true of God's people since long before the time of the apostles.

The English word *church* is a translation of the Greek word *ekklesia*, which means "called out." In the New Testament the word does not refer to a building, since it would be centuries until the first Christians worshipped special structures. Instead, the word refers to those people whom God has *called out of the world* to be his chosen people. The same word is used in the Greek translation of the Old Testament to refer to the sacred assembly of Israel, the people whom God first called out. Saint Stephen uses the word in his speech before his martyrdom when he says that Moses "was in the congregation (*ekklesia*) in the wilderness" (Acts 7:38).

Even if you have a spotty memory of Sunday school, you'll remember that God's chosen people in the Old Testament were constantly plagued with scandal. After Moses went up Mt. Sinai, the people began worshipping a golden calf that Aaron embarrassingly explained to Moses in the following way: "Moses, you know these people. They love false gods, so I just took their gold and threw it into a fire and then this golden calf just popped right out!" (at least, that's my loose translation of Exodus 32:21-24).

Or consider the book of Judges. It describes people whom God specifically "raised up" to deliver Israel from oppression. God probably doesn't choose a pope in the same way but allows the college of cardinals to do that. Pope Benedict XVI even said the Holy Spirit might only ensure the cardinals don't pick the worst pope, not that they will always pick the best pope![115] But when you look at Scripture it's clear God didn't pick "the best people" to lead Israel. For example:

- Gideon led God's people into idolatry by creating a golden Ephod they worshipped (Judg. 8:22-29).
- Samson visited a prostitute (Judg. 16:1-3) and broke Israel's ritual holiness laws (Judg. 14:6-9).
- Jephthah vowed to sacrifice a human being in order to win a battle and ended up sacrificing his own daughter (Judg. 11).

- Finally, though he wasn't a judge of Israel, the Bible calls Lot righteous (2 Pet. 2:7) and he served as a judge at the gates of Sodom. He offered his daughters to a rape-hungry mob (Gen. 19:8), and later got so drunk he ended up having intercourse with them (Gen. 19:30-38).

We could go on—and on not just with outright scandals, but also with the confusion that resulted from the leaders of God's chosen people failing to rebuke those causing evil and scandal in their midst. However, none of the scandals among the leaders of the chosen people in the Old Testament would have justified an Israelite throwing in the towel and trying to find salvation through Molech, Baal, or some worldly philosophy instead.

Or, to give a New Testament example, Peter caused so much scandal when he refused to dine with Gentile Christians that Paul had to publicly rebuke him (Gal. 2:14). But his actions did not justify leaving the apostolic church because Peter, the first pope, sent a confusing message with his actions that could have led some to think the Judaizing heretics were right about Gentile Christians not being "real Christians."

Next, we should also consider that claims of "embarrassing scandal" are often leveled at Catholicism in a way that unfairly carves out an escape hatch for Protestants, revealing a fatal problem in Protestantism's authority structure.

The Real Liberal Menace

I've met Lutherans and Anglicans who criticized Pope Francis for being orthodox on homosexuality one minute and then the next minute having a cheery photo op with a priest or theologian who causes confusion on the issue. They say that such actions erase any practical benefit Catholicism has for being the "living Magisterium" that guides believers to true doctrine. But I'd rather deal with the teaching office of Christ's Church making prudential errors in judgment than have to deal with denominations that hold wildly different views on key moral or doctrinal questions.

Other Protestants will claim that Catholicism cannot deliver on the benefits I outlined earlier in this book. They might say that the Magisterium has never infallibly defined the essential doctrines Catholics must believe, and so Protestants shouldn't be criticized for failing to have a similar list. Furthermore, there are still schismatics who call themselves "Catholic," so why should I be concerned about liberal Lutherans or Presbyterians giving "real, conservative Protestants" a bad name?

However, no one claims that an authoritative Magisterium allows Catholicism to completely avoid the problems of disunity afflicting Protestantism. Rather, Catholicism is the *least susceptible* to these problems, making it much more likely to be the fullest expression of the Christian faith.

Catholic bishops, even the liberal ones, agree about far more about essential and infallibly defined doctrines than do Protestant ministers and elders. Many of those doctrines are stated plainly in the canons of ecumenical councils, so there's little dispute over their formulation or meaning. Whereas Protestants can't even agree about something as fundamental as the recipients and mode of baptism, no similar disagreement exists among Catholic bishops. And any bishop who did practice unorthodox disciplines or espouse heretical views on something so fundamental would get an urgent letter from Rome inquiring about why they've created a canonical mess for themselves.

There *are* some parish communities that claim to be Catholic but hold heretical views. One would be the "Old Catholic

Church" that broke away from the true Catholic Church in the nineteenth century. Its members embrace an odd mixture of traditionalism and modern heresy, such as allowing contraception and even "gay marriage."[116] But these self-described (schismatic) Catholics are a negligible part of the global Catholic population and are easy to identify.

This stands in contrast to large liberal Protestant denominations, like the Evangelical Lutheran Church of America, that actually outnumber faithful denominations from the same tradition. And even conservative Protestants, who would say that liberal Protestants are being unfaithful to that Protestant tradition, themselves often hold views that would have gotten them burned at the stake in Calvin's Geneva or other Reformation strongholds of the sixteenth century.

One of the practical benefits that Catholic authority has over Protestantism is the unity that the pope provides by being able to teach universally or pronounce universal codifications of doctrine. And by defining "being Catholic" as recognizing the authority of the pope and the bishops in union with him, the Church avoids the problem of defining which denominations are truly Catholic and which are just Catholic in name only.

Just as none of these failures God's leaders in the Old Covenant disproved the truth that salvation is from the Jews (John 4:22), none of the failures of God's leaders in the New Covenant disprove the truth that salvation is from the Catholic Church.

OBJECTION 15:

Why Risk It?

"The Catholic Church teaches that Protestants can still be saved. So why become Catholic?"

"If I became Catholic, I'd lose everything."

As I continued to read this email, my heart broke for the Protestant pastor who sent it to me. He said he spent the last year reading the Church Fathers and studying Catholicism. He was now convinced the Catholic Church was the Church that Christ founded but he agonized over how to tell this to the congregation of the small Baptist church he led.

His wife already knew about his intentions and hated talking about it with him. She loved their church and even accused her husband of betraying their family. If he became Catholic, he would not only have to quit his job—he could never be a pastor again. How would he support his family if his Protestant seminary education became useless?

It's at this point that some Protestant apologists will say that since Catholics they talk to generally don't believe Protestants automatically go to hell for not converting, and since the Church in fact teaches that it is possible for a Protestant to go to heaven, then why not remain Protestant? Especially if conversion would be so costly.

But those same Protestant apologists have to answer a variant of this objection; and their reply shows how Catholics should respond to the "cost of conversion" objection.

The Conversion Dilemma

Some Protestants present this very dilemma for Catholics. If Protestants can go to heaven, then why bother becoming Catholic, especially if there's a high personal cost? Furthermore, if the only Protestants who go to hell are those who reject Catholicism openly and with full knowledge, then maybe Catholics shouldn't share their faith with Protestants at all, so that they remain in a safe kind of ignorance.

But in fact, all Christians face this same dilemma when it comes to evangelization. An atheist can ask a Protestant, "Do all non-Christians go to hell?" A simple yes answer seems cruel. If, then, non-Christians *can* go to heaven, why should anyone bother to become Christian? And why try to convince anyone to become Christian? Maybe ignorance of Christianity would be safer for their souls.

Let's look at how Protestants answer this challenge and how it might apply to the Catholic version of this objection.

First, there are the *exclusivist* Protestants. Their beliefs exist on a spectrum that tends to be pessimistic toward the salvation of those who never accept Christianity, including those who never even heard of Christ. Some exclusivists even claim flatly that anyone who never heard of Christ, including children in Christian families who die in infancy, cannot enter heaven.

When pressed with the seeming cruelty of their view, they will say we cannot judge God but can only abide by what he has revealed. If God revealed that faith in Christ is absolutely required for salvation, then we mere creatures should tremble before his just decrees. And for them, even if someone claims to love Jesus but is in grave theological error (e.g. Mormons, Oneness Pentecostals), such a person cannot be saved because doesn't have faith in the true Jesus.

An exclusivist Catholic could simply tell an exclusivist Protestant: God has revealed that we must be in union with him and his Church to be saved. God gave us sacraments like baptism and the Eucharist that are necessary for eternal life, and we can't reject them. Who are you to tell God who he will and will not save from their sins?

An exclusivist Protestant might reply that the Catholic Church is in error about what God requires for salvation, but he can't say the Catholic is being cruel. He may in fact believe that *Catholics* will go to hell for their false theology, so he shouldn't clutch his pearls over the notion that the same fate awaits Protestants who reject Christ's Church.

The Catholic Church, meanwhile, holds to a more inclusivist view of salvation toward non-Catholics, a view that can resonate with Protestants who hold a similar view toward non-Christians.

Possible but Not Probable Salvation

The idea expressed in the Latin phrase *extra ecclesiam nulla salus*, "outside the Church there is no salvation," has been taught for centuries. In 1215, the Fourth Lateran Council taught, "There is one universal Church of the faithful, outside of which there is absolutely no salvation." But the Church has never infallibly taught that this means that only Catholics, or even only Christians, can be saved. The teaching has developed over the centuries to communicate the truth that, if someone is saved, he is saved only through the work of Jesus Christ (Acts 4:12) and his body, the Church (Eph. 5:25-27). But even the first Christians recognized that Christ could save people who, through no fault of their own, failed to accept him or his Church.

Paul wrote about pagans who did not know the Old Testament law who would be judged according to the law written on their hearts, their *conscience* (Rom. 2:14). In the second century, Justin Martyr wrote, "We have been taught that Christ is the first-born of God, and we have declared above that he is the Word of whom every race of men were partakers; and those who lived reasonably are Christians, even though they have been thought atheists; as, among the Greeks, Socrates and Heraclitus, and men like them."[117] And St. Augustine said, "If unbaptized persons die confessing Christ, this confession is of the same efficacy for the remission of sins as if they were washed in the sacred font of baptism."[118]

These early Christians recognized how someone could be united to Christ in his soul even if he lacked the ordinary means of creating this union, such as baptism or even faith, because he was ignorant of Christ through no fault of his own. During the Middle Ages, theologians used narrower language to describe who could be saved because they thought that the entire world had been evangelized and only the remaining non-Christians were those who stubbornly refused to accept the truth. However, after the discovery of people in the New World, the Church further developed its understanding of the possibility of salvation for non-Catholics. It made a distinction between *vincible* ignorance that could have been overcome through due diligence and *invincible* ignorance that could not have been overcome.

Examples of the former would be willfully refusing to accept your intellect's conclusion that Christianity is true or choosing not to study the evidence for the Faith because you're afraid it will lead you to convert. Examples of the latter would be being born in a place that Christian missionaries had not yet reached or having heard only false or deficient proclamations of the gospel.

In the seventeenth century, Cardinal Juan de Lugo of Spain said indigenous people even in Catholic colonies could still be invincibly ignorant of the Faith because of the cruel actions of the colonizers who "evangelized" them. Through abusive treatment and poor catechesis, they caused the indigenous people reject a hypocritical counterfeit Catholicism—not the true Faith that condemned how they were being mistreated.

And so, a person can be invincibly ignorant of the Faith, even if he has heard the facts about it, because he lacks a proper *understanding* of it. A person whose only knowledge of Christianity comes from caricatures in online atheist memes, for instance, or a Protestant who has only heard from his church that the pope is the Antichrist, will be less culpable for his ignorance. This understanding culminated in the twentieth century with the Second Vatican Council's teaching that

> those also can attain to salvation who through no fault of their own do not know the gospel of Christ or his Church, yet sincerely seek God and moved by grace strive by their deeds to do his will as it is known to them through the dictates of conscience. Nor does divine Providence deny the helps necessary for salvation to those who, without blame on their part, have not yet arrived at an explicit knowledge of God and with his grace strive to live a good life (*Lumen Gentium* 16).

This does not mean salvation is guaranteed, or even probable, for those who do not know Christ. It just means it is *possible*, which is why that same passage of *Lumen Gentium* adds that, because men often succumb to sin and despair, "the Church fosters the missions with care and attention." So, the Church believes in evangelism without embracing an *exclusivism* that denies the universal potential of God's saving power. And this applies both to those who have not yet accepted the divine identity of Jesus Christ and those who have not yet accepted the divine authority of Christ's Church.

Leaving Everything to Follow Him

What inclusivist Protestants believe about the possibility of salvation for non-Christians is analogous to what Catholics believe about the possibility of salvation for non-Catholics: salvation is a possibility but not one we should simply assume; which is why we should still share our faith and why sharing it doesn't endanger those with whom we share it. They also acknowledge that is a difference between someone who isn't Catholic or even Christian through no fault of his own (invincible ignorance) and someone who rejects Christ and/or his church because he doesn't want to hear or believe the truth. Cardinal de Lugo made this point, too:

> One who is baptized as an infant by heretics, and is brought up by them in false doctrine, when he reaches adulthood, could for some time not be guilty of sin against the Catholic faith, as long as this had not been proposed to him in a way sufficient to oblige him to embrace it. However, if the Catholic faith were subsequently proposed to him in a way sufficient to oblige him to embrace it and to abandon errors contrary to it, and he still persisted in his errors, then he would be a heretic.[119]

But if someone knows that God wants him to believe that Jesus is God or that the Eucharist at Mass is truly Jesus, and he chooses to not accept that truth or act in accord with it, then he puts his soul in danger. This is even true of someone who doesn't *yet* know that God wants him to believe these doctrines, but who sinfully rejects ways of coming to know the truth because he'd prefer to live in ignorance.

The Catholic Church recognizes that many Protestants, by virtue of their valid baptisms, have an imperfect communion with Christ's Church.[120] As Catholics, we desire that all people accept the gospel, and that all who accept it be brought into perfect communion with the Church, whose ministers are the successors of the apostles and by their teaching authority guide believers to salvation.

All this is why I asked that pastor worried about losing his job, "What would you tell a Muslim imam or a Jewish rabbi who wanted to become Christian? Or even one who is at least open to Christianity?"

Perhaps he'd quote the words of our Lord to Peter: "Truly, I say to you, there is no one who has left house or brothers or sisters or mother or father or children or lands, for my sake and for the gospel, who will not receive a hundredfold now in this time, houses and brothers and sisters and mothers and children and lands, with persecutions, and in the age to come eternal life" (Mark 10:29–30).

Conclusion

My four-year-old son Matthew smiled as the waves splashed against his feet, but his hands still dug into my skin as we waded out into the ocean. Small waves lapped against my stomach as I pointed out fish swimming around us. Matt was still getting used to the water and couldn't swim, but he always felt safe when I held him.

I looked back and smiled at my wife holding our other son, wondering if she could see how excited Matthew was to be out in the water. But when I turned back to the horizon, my stomach dropped.

The tiny waves that had barely reached my chest now combined into one large swell that towered over us. I tried to run back to the beach, but my legs felt like they were moving through molasses in the waist-deep water. When the wave hit, it felt like someone punched me in the back of the head, and I felt the water squeeze Matthew out of my arms.

After the wave passed, I stood up and frantically scanned the once-clear water that was now covered in sea foam. "Matthew!" I screamed at the top of my lungs.

A second later he shot up from under the water like a cork, thanks to the life jacket he was wearing. But that second had felt like an eternity as I wondered if his life jacket had come off and he was drowning right in front of me.

I scooped him up and said, "Are you okay, big guy?"

He coughed. "I was spinning around and around and then I said, 'I better push my feet and go up' and then I did and now I'm okay."

I proceeded to give him what is now probably the third-biggest hug he's ever received in his life.

A few weeks later, I was on a plane traveling to a conference, and my seatmate was asking me about my family and my faith. She admitted she wasn't religious, but she was interested in learning about Catholicism, so I shared with her how my faith has blessed my family and me. I also told her about my recent scary incident at the ocean.

"I don't mean to be grim," she intoned, "But what if your son had died? What would you have done?"

I took a breath and replied to her not as a Catholic apologist, but as a father:

"I don't know. I don't even want to think about it. I wouldn't be surprised if I ended up in a very dark place. But I would never do anything that could jeopardize the one thing I have that would let me see my son again in heaven. I would never give up the salvation I have in Jesus Christ and his Church."

I'm grateful that nothing tragic happened to my family that day at the beach. But for some people, the story turns out very differently, and their hope in God's promises of eternal life is put to the ultimate test. And even if we never know the tragedy of losing a child, eventually each of us will face the final moment we draw breath in this mortal life.

The doctrine of salvation isn't a theological game or interesting thought experiment for religious hobbyists to debate. It is a matter of life and death, which is why I wrote this book. I wrote it to share with every single person why unending life with God comes through Christ's one, holy, catholic, and apostolic church.

As we've seen, the Catholic Church saves us through at least ten different ways:

1. Defining what God has revealed
2. Teaching us how to obey God
3. Consecrating the flesh and blood of Christ
4. Leading proper worship of God
5. Baptizing unbelievers
6. Absolving believers of sin
7. Uniting us to Christ's bride
8. Uniting us with Peter's successor
9. Giving us spiritual reinforcements
10. Confirming itself with signs and wonders

The simplest way to say no to God's offer of salvation is to completely reject Christ and to leave the Faith entirely. Peter says it would be better for Christians never to have "known the way of righteousness than after knowing it to turn back from the holy commandment delivered to them" (2 Pet. 2:21). In commenting on this passage, Martin Luther said, "Through baptism these people threw out unbelief, had their unclean way of life washed away, and entered into a pure life of faith and love. Now they fall away into unbelief and . . . soil themselves again in filth."[121]

But we can also forsake Christ through our actions even if we say we are faithful to him with our words—like how an adulterous husband forsakes his wife through his actions even if he tells her, "I love you." Remember the haunting words of Christ that some self-described Christians will hear at the last judgment: "Not every one who says to me, 'Lord, Lord,' shall enter the kingdom of heaven, but he who does the will of my Father who is in heaven" (Matt. 7:21).

To avoid forsaking Jesus, a Christian must not die in a state of grave sin, of which we can speak of two types:

1. Freely choosing to perform a gravely evil act
2. Freely choosing not to perform an obligatory good act

When we think of grave sins, we usually think of the first type: acts of evil we choose to do that we know we shouldn't (sins of *commission*). A summary list of such acts, based on the Ten Commandments, might look like this:

> Apostasy, heresy, idolatry, superstition, occultism, blasphemy, dishonoring parents and legitimate authorities, murder, abortion, euthanasia, hatred, abuse, slander, injurious gossip, drunkenness, gluttony, lust, fornication or sexual stimulation outside of marriage, adultery, pornography, prostitution, rape, contraception, sterilization, IVF, gestational surrogacy, masturbation, sodomy, bestiality, grave theft, wage theft, tax fraud, cultivated envy, grave lies, perjury.

Catholic and Protestants agree that we must not commit gravely evil acts, even though we disagree about whether it is possible for a "true Christian" to unrepentantly commit these grave acts. In this book we've seen that it is legitimate, terrifying possibility that our Lord himself warned us about.

The more challenging divide between Catholics and Protestants seems to be over not which grave evils we must not do, but *which good things are we obligated to do*—or to put it another way, what constitutes grave sins of *omission.*

James 4:17 says, "Whoever knows what is right to do and fails to do it, for him it is sin." The Catholic Church teaches that Christians have the following duties they must fulfill, which are called the precepts of the Church (CCC 2041-2043):

1. Attend Mass on Sundays and holy days of obligation
2. Receive the Eucharist at least once a year
3. Confess your mortal sins at least once a year
4. Observe days of fasting and abstinence
5. Support the Church's needs (according to one's ability)

These precepts aren't tasks that earn us salvation. Rather, they are God's way of helping us live the Christian life because he knows we are in the battle for our lives. That's why Paul says this in Ephesians,

> Put on the whole armor of God, that you may be able to stand against the wiles of the devil. For we are not contending against flesh and blood, but against the principalities, against the powers, against the world rulers of this present darkness, against the spiritual hosts of wickedness in the heavenly places. Therefore take the whole armor of God, that you may be able to withstand in the evil day, and having done all, to stand (Eph. 6:11-13).

Some Catholic practices are mandatory for the good of our souls, like attending Mass or going to confession and receiving the Eucharist at least once a year. They also include fasting on days like Ash Wednesday or Good Friday, because God knows we are better able to say no to the devil when we practice saying no to the flesh. Similarly, the practice of "providing for the material needs of the Church, each according to his abilities" (CCC 2043) makes us better able to say no to material excess and the temptations of wealth.

Many Protestants believe that a "true Christian" will attend church, celebrate the Lord's Supper (however much it's offered), and confess particularly grave sins to God. Throughout this book, we've seen that only the Catholic Church has the authority and the ability to help us follow Jesus' salvific commands to "eat his flesh" (John 6:53) and the apostle's teaching to "confess our sins to one another" (Jas. 5:16) in the context of the Church's priests.

I sometimes ask Protestants who are open to becoming Catholic but remain hesitant, "What do you have to lose?" If they say, "My salvation," I remind them that this simple fear shows they aren't saved by faith alone, since to be saved you apparently also have to do the "good work" of not becoming Catholic. But that would disprove *sola fide*, the belief in justification by faith alone. This dilemma further confirms the need for an authoritative church to fully answer the perennial question, "What must I do to be saved?"

Finally, we saw that other Catholic practices may not be strictly necessary for our salvation, but they are still good because they strengthen us for the trials of this life. The Church has been blessed with so many devotions and examples of saintly prayer and habits that no one could incorporate all of them into his or her spiritual life. Since people are unique, each of us will be attracted to different kinds of devotions or private rituals (e.g. the rosary, the Liturgy of the Hours, etc.) that help us to grow in our faith. And many of these devotions are small but helpful, like saying the sign of the cross to always remind ourselves of the graces we received in baptism.

If you are a non-Catholic, I invite you to inquire more about the saving grace freely offered to you through the universal church of Jesus Christ. I think you'll find, as I have, that the Catholic Church's plan of salvation brings an enduring peace to your soul and rings out in perfect harmony with the promise of our Savior Jesus Christ:

"Come to me, all who labor and are heavy laden, and I will give you rest. Take my yoke upon you, and learn from me; for I am gentle and lowly in heart, and you will find rest for your souls." (Matt 11:28-30).

APPENDIX I

How to Become Catholic

All people are brought into full communion with the Catholic Church through reception of the three sacraments of Christian initiation: baptism, confirmation, and the Eucharist. But the *process* by which someone becomes a Catholic can take different forms.

A person who is baptized in the Catholic Church becomes a Catholic at that moment. This initiation is deepened by confirmation and the Eucharist, but one is a Catholic from the moment of baptism. This is true for children who are baptized Catholic and receive the other two sacraments later as well as for adults who are baptized, confirmed, and receive the Eucharist at the same time.

Those who have been validly baptized outside the Church become Catholics by making a profession of the Catholic faith and being formally received into the Church. This is normally followed immediately by confirmation and the Eucharist.

Before a person is ready to be received into the Church, whether by baptism or by profession of faith, preparation is necessary. The amount and form of this preparation depends on the individual's circumstance. The most basic division in the kind of preparation needed is between those who are unbaptized and those who have already become Christian through baptism in another church or Christian community.

Steps to Becoming Catholic for the Unbaptized

Preparation for reception into the Church for those above the age of reason (age seven) begins with the *inquiry stage*, in which the unbaptized person begins to learn about the Catholic faith and decide whether to embrace it.

The first formal step to becoming Catholic begins with the *rite of reception* into the *order of catechumens*, in which the unbaptized express their desire and intention to become Christians. *Catechumen* is a term the early Christians used to refer to those preparing to be baptized.

The period of the *catechumenate* varies depending on how much the catechumen has learned and how ready he feels to take the step of becoming a Christian. Typically, though, it lasts less than a year.

The catechumenate's purpose is to provide catechumens with a thorough background in Christian teaching. It is also intended to give catechumens the opportunity to reflect upon and become firm in their desire to become Catholic.

The second formal step is taken with the *rite of election*, in which the catechumens' names are written in a book of those who will receive the sacraments of initiation. At the rite of election, the catechumen again expresses the desire and intention to become a Christian, and the Church judges that the catechumen is ready to take this step. Normally, the rite of election occurs on the first Sunday of Lent, the forty-day period of preparation for Easter.

After the rite of election, the candidates undergo a period of more intense reflection, purification, and enlightenment, in which they deepen their commitment to repentance and conversion. During this period, the catechumens, now known as the *elect*, participate in several further rituals.

The three chief rituals, known as *scrutinies*, are normally celebrated at Mass on the third, fourth, and fifth Sundays of Lent. The scrutinies are rites for self-searching and repentance. They are meant to bring out the qualities of the catechumen's soul, to heal those qualities that are weak or sinful, and to strengthen those that are positive and good.

During this period, the catechumens are formally presented with the Apostles' Creed and the Lord's Prayer, which they will recite on the night they are initiated.

The initiation itself usually occurs on the Easter Vigil, the evening before Easter Day. That evening, a special Mass is celebrated at which the catechumens are baptized, then given confirmation, and finally receive the Holy Eucharist. At this point, the catechumens have become Catholics and are received into full communion with the Church.

Sometimes, the bishop oversees the Easter Vigil and confers confirmation upon the catechumens, but often—due to large distances or numbers of catechumens—a parish priest will perform the rites.

The final state of Christian initiation is known as *mystagogy*, in which the new Catholics are strengthened in the Faith by further instruction and become more deeply rooted in the local Catholic community. The period of mystagogy normally lasts throughout the Easter season (the fifty days between Easter and Pentecost Sunday).

For the first year of their life as Christians, those who have been received are known as *neophytes* or "new Christians."

Preparation for the Already Baptized

The means by which those who have already been validly baptized become part of the Church are somewhat different. Because they have already been baptized, these people are already Christians; they are, therefore, not called catechumens.

For those who were baptized but who have never been instructed in the Christian faith or lived as Christians, it is appropriate for them to receive much of the same instruction in the Faith as catechumens do, even though they do not participate in the rites intended for catechumens, such as the scrutinies. Prior to their reception into full communion with the Church, those baptized persons who *have* been instructed in Christian teachings and have lived as Christians are instructed in the Catholic tradition to supplement their knowledge of the Faith and its practice.

Peace with God

The sacrament of baptism removes all sins committed prior to it, but since Christians have already been baptized, it is necessary for them to confess mortal sins committed since baptism before receiving confirmation and the Eucharist. They do this to ensure that they are in a *state of grace* when they are received and confirmed.

In some cases, this can be difficult, due to a large number of years between the Christian's baptism and his reception into the Catholic Church. In such cases, the candidate should strive at least to confess the mortal sins he can remember by kind and, to the extent possible, indicate how often such sins were committed. As always with the sacrament of reconciliation, the absolution given covers all mortal sins, even those that could not be remembered, as long as the recipient intended to repent of all mortal sins.

The Christian fully enters the Church by a profession of faith and formal rite of reception. For the profession of faith, the candidate says, "I believe and profess all that the holy

Catholic Church believes, teaches, and proclaims to be revealed by God."

The bishop or priest then formally receives the Christian into the Church by saying, "[Name], the Lord receives you into the Catholic Church. His loving kindness has led you here, so that in the unity of the Holy Spirit you may have full communion with us in the faith that you have professed in the presence of his family."

The bishop or priest then normally administers the sacrament of confirmation and celebrates the Holy Eucharist, giving the new Catholic the Eucharist for the first time.

Reception in Special Cases

In some situations, there may be doubts whether a person's baptism was valid. All Christian baptisms are presumed valid, unless after serious investigation there is reason to doubt that the candidate was baptized with water and the trinitarian formula ("in the name of the Father and of the Son and of the Holy Spirit"), or that the minister or recipient of baptism did not intend it to be an actual baptism.

If there are doubts about the validity of a person's baptism, the candidate will be given a *conditional* baptism: "If you are not already baptized, I baptize you in the name of the Father and of the Son and of the Holy Spirit."

Another special case concerns those who have been baptized as Catholics but who were not brought up in the Faith or who have not received the sacraments of confirmation and the Eucharist. Such people will receive a formation fitted to their circumstance.

Those candidates who are Christians already have, by virtue of their baptism, a certain sacramental relationship with the Church (*Unitatis Redintegratio* 3; CCC 1271). They are also joined to the Church by their intention to enter it, as are the unbaptized who intend to do so: "Catechumens who, moved by the Holy Spirit, desire with an explicit intention to be incorporated into the Church are by that very intention joined to her. With love and solicitude mother Church already embraces them as her own" (*Lumen Gentium* 14). Completing this relationship and sealing that intention by formal reception into full communion is for candidates and catechumens a moment of great joy and grace.

APPENDIX II

The Examination of Conscience

An examination of conscience is a reflective exercise in which you assess your thoughts, words, and deeds in light of the Church's moral teachings to prepare yourself for the sacrament of confession. It also serves as a means of spiritual growth, ongoing conversion, and personal renewal. Through carefully considering the guidance provided by the Ten Commandments, the Beatitudes, Catholic moral teaching, and Scripture, a sincere examination of conscience helps you develop a deeper awareness of your spiritual state and a genuine desire to repent and remain with the Lord.

There are four essential steps to making an examination of conscience.

Step One: Choose a resource tailored to your state of life.

There are many written resources available, in print form as well as online, modern and traditional, to guide you in examining your conscience. When discerning which examination of conscience to use, it's prudent to consider your state of life—age, marital status, vocation, and so on. All these will recommend different emphases on moral obligations and spiritual disciplines. Pick one that fits you.

Step Two: Find a place to reflect and pray.

Seek out a quiet and comfortable space to reflect, whether at home, outdoors in nature, or at church while waiting to enter the confessional. Turn off your phone and allow yourself to be free from all distractions. The setting for your examination of conscience should promote interior peace and the ability to concentrate.

Step Three: Pray for God's aid.

Before embarking on your examination of conscience, it is important to cultivate humility and openness to God's grace. Begin with prayer, invoking the Holy Spirit to illuminate your conscience and guide your reflections. Approach this spiritual exercise with sincerity and honesty, recognizing your ongoing need for conversion and spiritual growth. Here is an example of a prayer you can use:

> Come Holy Spirit into my soul, enlighten my mind that I may know the sins I ought to confess, and grant me your grace to confess them fully, humbly, and with a contrite heart. Help me to firmly resolve not to commit them again. O Blessed Virgin, mother of my Redeemer, mirror of innocence and sanctity, and refuge of penitent sinners, intercede for me through the passion of your son, that I may obtain the grace to make a good confession. All you blessed angels and saints of God, pray for me, a most miserable sinner, that I may repent of my evil ways, that my heart may henceforth be forever united with yours in eternal love. Amen.

Step Four: Read and pray through your examination.

Take your time. Don't rush through the words in your head; instead, read them multiple times and even say them with your lips if it helps you to focus. Be honest with yourself and with God as you reflect on your failings and weaknesses. Seek neither to excuse yourself of your faults nor to dwell on them excessively. God's mercy is ready, and it is inexhaustible for those who approach him in humility.

> Be ashamed when you sin, not when you repent.
>
> —St. John Chrysostom

About the Author

After his conversion to the Catholic faith, Trent Horn earned master's degrees in the fields of theology, philosophy, and bioethics. He serves as a staff apologist for Catholic Answers, where he specializes in teaching Catholics to graciously and persuasively engage those who disagree with them. Trent models that approach each week on the radio program *Catholic Answers Live* and on his own podcast, *The Counsel of Trent.* He has also been invited to debate at UC Berkeley, UC Santa Barbara, and Stanford University. Trent is an adjunct professor of apologetics at Holy Apostles College, has written for *The National Catholic Bioethics Quarterly*, and is the author of nine books, including *Answering Atheism*, *The Case for Catholicism*, and *Why We're Catholic: Our Reasons for Faith, Hope, and Love.*

Endnotes

1 See "Relationship between Jesus Christ and Satan" at https://www.fairlatterdaysaints.org/answers/Jesus_Christ/Brother_of_Satan.

2 J. Grescham Machen, *The Virgin Birth of Christ* (London: Marshall, Morgan, and Scott, 1930), 395.

3 Ibid, 396.

4 Protestant author Gavin Ortlund acknowledges Catholic and Protestant persecution of the anabaptists, saying, "There were probably more anabaptist martyrs in the sixteenth century than Christian martyrs in the first three centuries of the church." Gavin Ortlund, *Finding the Right Hills to Die On: The Case for Theological Triage* (Wheaton, IL: Crossway, 2020), 100. During the Reformation, the prominent Lutheran theologian Philip Melancthon said of the anabaptists that "the stubborn sectaries must be put to death." Johannes Janssen, *History of the German People from the Close of the Middle Ages*, vol. 10 (St. Louis: B. Herder, 1910), 222-223.

5 Dale Chamberlain, "Southern Baptists Do Not Adopt Nicene Creed at Annual Meeting" *Church Leaders* (June 14, 2024), Available online at: https://churchleaders.com/news/487608-southern-baptists-do-not-adopt-nicene-creed-at-annual-meeting.html/2.

6 Jaroslav Pelikan, *The Christian Tradition: A History of the Development of Doctrine*, vol. 1, *The Emergence of the Catholic Tradition (100-600)* (Chicago: University of Chicago Press, 1971), 148.

7 Craig Blomberg, *1 Corinthians: The NIV Application Commentary* (Grand Rapids, MI: Zondervan, 1994), 130.

8 Quoted in J. Verres, *Luther: An Historical Portrait* (New York: Burns and Oates, 1884), 313. Original source: De Wette II, 459.

9 "Is Abortion a Catholic Issue?" Christianity Today, (January 16, 1976). Available online at: https://www.christianitytoday.com/ct/1976/january-16/editorials-is-abortion-catholic-issue.html

10 See Christopher B. Hays and Richard B. Hays, *The Widening of God's Mercy: Sexuality Within the Biblical Story* (2024).

11 Tara John, Catherine Nicholls and Christopher Lamb, "Pope calls for ban on surrogacy, calling it 'based on exploitation,'" CNN.com (January 8, 2024), https://edition.cnn.com/2024/01/08/world/pope-ban-surrogacy.

12 *First Apology*, 15.

13 A. Andrew Das, *Remarriage in Early Christianity* (Grand Rapids: Wm. Eerdmans, 2024), 434.

14 "The wife, if she leaves her husband and goes to another, is an adulteress. But the man who has been abandoned is pardonable, and the woman who lives with such a man is not condemned." *Letter* 188.

15 Homily on Matthew, 62.

16 "Divorce and Remarriage," available online at: https://www.oca.org/questions/sacramentmarriage/divorce-and-remarriage.

17 Tikhon Alexander Pino, *Contraception and the Orthodox Church* (Patristic Nectar Publications, 2025), 13-14.

18 John Meyendorff, *Marriage: An Orthodox Perspective* (Crestwood: St. Vladimir's Seminary Press, 1984), 61.

19 "Synodal Affirmations on Marriage, Family, Sexuality, and the Sanctity of Life" Available online at: https://www.oca.org/holy-synod/%20statements/holy-synod/synodal-affirmations-on-marriage-family-sexuality-and-the-sanctity-of-life.

20 Epistle to the Smyrnaeans, 7.

21 *First Apology*, 15.

22 Darwell Stone, *The Holy Communion* (London: Longmans, Green, 1904), 37.

23 Joachim Jeremias, *The Eucharistic Words of Jesus* (New York: Charles Scribner and Sons, 1966).

24 Martin Luther, *Works of Luther: With Introductions and Notes*, ed. Henry Eyster Jacobs and Adolph Spaeth (Philadelphia: A. J. Holman, 1915), 213.

25 Some Protestants say this obligation is found in Hebrews 10:24-25: "Let us consider how to stir up one another to love and good works, not neglecting to meet together, as is the habit of some, but encouraging one another, and all the more as you see the Day drawing near." But the verse says nothing about these meetings needing to be weekly, with the entire congregation, taking place on Sunday, at church. A simple Bible study could meet this requirement. Protestants also assume that this is a perpetually binding command rather than a prudent custom, including a custom that doesn't apply today, such as Paul's rules on veiling in 1 Corinthians 11. Although it lends support to the practice of obligatory weekly worship, this verse does not prove such an obligation.

26 D.A. Carson, "Worship Under the Word", in *Worship by the Book*, ed. D.A. Carson (Grand Rapids, MI: Zondervan, 2002), 26.

27 *City of God*, 10.4.

28 O.S. Hawkins, *The Pastor's Primer* (Guidestone Financial Resources, 2009), 31.

29 *First Apology*, 66.

30 Ibid., 61.

31 Oscar Cullmann, *Baptism in the New Testament*, Studies in Biblical Theology, no. 1 (London: SCM Press, 1950), 11.

32 Martin Luther, *Large Catechism*, "Holy Baptism."

33 *Didache*, 7.

34 Hippolytus, *The Apostolic Tradition* 21.4. Translation found in Gregory Dix and Henry Chadwick, *The Treatise on the Apostolic Tradition of St Hippolytus of Rome, Bishop and Martyr* (New York: Routledge, 2006; original publishing, 1937), 33.

35 St. Cyprian, Letters, 64.5.

36 Origen, *Commentary on Romans* 5.9. This translation can be found in Thomas Scheck, *Origen: Commentary on the Epistle to the Romans Books 1–5* (Washington, DC: Catholic University of America Press, 2001), 367.

37 R.C. Sproul, *What Is Baptism?* (Grand Rapids, MI: Reformation Trust Publishing, 2011), 68.

38 *Concerning Repentance*, 1.8.

39 *On the Priesthood,* 3.5.

40 *Against Heresies*, 1.13.

41 *The Lapsed,* 29.

42 Ibid., 28.

43 Epistle to the Smyrnaeans, 8.

44 *Against Heresies*, 3.4.1.

45 1 Clement, 44.

46 Craig Keener, *Acts: An Exegetical Commentary, vol. 2, 3:1-14:28* (Grand Rapids, MI: Baker Academic, 2013).

47 Epistle to the Smyrnaeans, 8.

48 Epistle to the Trallians, 3.

49 D.A. Carson, "Church Authority," in *Evangelical Dictionary of Theology*, 2nd ed. (Grand Rapids, MI: Baker, 2001), 250. Carson says, "One reads of churches in Galatia [a region, not a city] but of the church in Antioch or Jerusalem or Ephesus."

50 Epistle to the Philadelphians, 3-4.

51 *Calvin's Genevan Ecclesiastical Ordinances*, 1541.

52 "The Consistory of Geneva, 1559-1569," *Bibliothèque d'Humanisme et Renaissance*, 38 (1976): 467-484. Cited in David Anders, "How John Calvin Made me a Catholic" Called to Communion (June 1, 2010), available online at: https://www.calledtocommunion.com/2010/06/how-john-calvin-made-me-a-catholic/

53 *Institutes of the Christian Religion*, 4.12.9.

54 *Epistle* 73.11.

55 *On the Unity of the Church*, 4.

56 J.N.D. Kelly, *Oxford Dictionary of the Popes* (New York: Oxford University Press, 1986), 1.

57 *Against Heresies*, 3.3.2.

58 Epistle 54.14.

59 Epistle 53.2.

60 *On Repentance*, 7.33.

61 Letter 15 to Pope Damasus, 2.

62 William Barclay, *The Letter to the Hebrews* (Louisville, KY: Westminster John Knox Press, 2002), 202.

63 *Of the Crown*, 3. Cited in C. Dodgson, *Tertullian Vol. 1. Apologetic and Practical Treatises* (1842).

64 *On the Incarnation of the Word*, 48.

65 Hector Avalos, *The End of Biblical Studies* (Amherst, NY: Prometheus Books, 2007), 193.

66 Richard Dawkins, *The God Delusion* (New York: Bantam Press, 2006), 91.

67 "Then he would seem to 'rise and float.' I would wager that he mimed this by stretching himself upward until he artfully stood on tiptoe, then danced lightly in place so as to create the illusion of 'hovering' just above the ground." Joe Nickell, "Secrets of 'The Flying Friar': Did St. Joseph of Copertino Really Levitate?," *Skeptical Inquirer*, vol. 42, no. 4 (July/August 2018).

68 *City of God*, 22.8

69 *Summa Contra Gentiles*, 1.6.1

70 John Calvin, *Institutes of the Christian Religion*, prefatory address.

71 B.B. Warfield, *Counterfeit Miracles* (New York: Charles Scribner's Sons, 1918), 66.

72 L. Philip Bames, "Miracles, Charismata and Benjamin B. Warfield," *Evangelical Quaterly* 67 no. 3 (1995).

73 *Essay on Miracles*, 2.4

74 Ibid.

75 Tyler McNabb and Joseph Blado, "Mary and Fátima: A Modest C-Inductive Argument for Catholicism" *Perichoresis* 18.5 (2020), 62.

76 Trent Horn, *Why We're Catholic: Our Reasons for Faith, Hope, and Love* (San Diego, CA: Catholic Answers Press, 2014), 65.

77 Council of Trent, Decree on Justification, 8.

78 Martin Luther, *Commentary on Galatians.*

79 Dale Moody, *The Word of Truth: A Summary of Christian Doctrine Based on Biblical Revelation* (Grand Rapids, MI: Wm. B. Eerdmans, 1981), 356.

80 See John Jefferson Davis, "The Perseverance of the Saints: A History of the Doctrine," *Journal of the Evangelical Theological Society* 34, no. 2 (June 1991): 214.

81 *Against Heresies*, 41.4.3.

82 *On Repentance*, 6.

83 St. Augustine, *Treatise on Rebuke and Grace*, 9.

84 Peter Lillback, "Eternal Security and the Early Saints" *Testamentum Imperium*, vol. 1, 2005-2007, 13.

85 James R. White, *Drawn by the Father* (Lindenhurst, NY: Great Christian Books, 2000), 26.

86 As I note in my book *The Case for Catholicism*, one could argue that Judas, or the Son of Perdition, was never a true believer and so his salvation was not lost. But this muddles Jesus' contrast of "losing" Judas in order to fulfill the Scriptures with his faithfulness in not "losing" the other apostles. If Judas were not at one point in a state of grace like the other apostles, then the comparison doesn't make sense. Moreover, in Matthew 19:28 Jesus says to the apostles, "You who have followed me will also sit on twelve thrones, judging the twelve tribes of Israel." According to Arie Zwiep in his monograph on Judas, "It makes no sense to apply the saying to a larger number of followers of Jesus, let alone to all believers. Originally, it was surely addressed to the twelve apostles." Arie W. Zwiep, *Judas and the Choice of Matthias: A Study on Context and Concern of Acts 1:15–26* (Heidelberg: Mohr Siebeck, 2004), 51.

87 Ben Witherington, *John's Wisdom: A Commentary on the Fourth Gospel* (Louisville, KY: Westminster John Knox Press, 1995), 158.

88 Scott Hahn, "Hunt for the Fourth Cup," *Catholic Answers Magazine* (September, 1, 1991).

89 "It must be noted that these ordinances, probably inspired by the customs of the period, concern scarcely more than disciplinary practices of minor importance, such as the obligation imposed upon women to wear a veil on their head (1 Cor 11:2-16); such requirements no longer have a normative value." *Inter Insigniores*, 4.

90 B.J. Oropeza, *Jews, Gentiles, and the Opponents of Paul: Apostasy in the New Testament Communities, vol. 2, The Pauline Letters* (Eugene, OR: Wipf and Stock, 2012), 219.

91 Pope Benedict XVI, General Audience (November 19, 2008).

92 *Commentary on The Gospel of Matthew*, 8.

93 Bart D. Ehrman, *Peter, Paul and Mary Magdalene: The Followers of Jesus in History and Legend* (New York: Oxford University Press, 2006), 167.

94 Jimmy Akin, *The Drama of Salvation* (San Diego: California, 2015), 52.

95 Ibid., 56.

96 Trent Horn, *The Case for Catholicism: Answers to Classic and Contemporary Protestant Objections* (San Francisco: Ignatius Press, 2017), 227.

97 St. Augustine, On Faith and Works 14.21. Cited in St. Augustine, *On Faith and Works*, trans. Gregory Lombardo (Paulist Press, 1988), 28.

98 *Luther's Works*, 54:49–50.

99 *On Faith and Works*, 22.

100 Jimmy Akin, *A Daily Defense* (San Diego: Catholic Answers Press, 2016), 261.

101 Thomas R. Schreiner, *Faith Alone—The Doctrine of Justification* (Grand Rapids, MI: Zondervan, 2015), 205.

102 Jimmy Akin, *A Daily Defense* (San Diego: Catholic Answers Press, 2016), 261.

103 Institutes of Elenctic Theology, 2:354.

104 Robert Wilkin, *Confident in Christ* (Irving, TX: Grace Evangelical Society, 1999), 29.

105 *Handbook on Faith, Hope, and Love*, 41.

106 When he was defending the importance of Christ's humanity in the atonement, Calvin wrote the following: "Although Christ could neither purify our souls by his own blood, nor appease the Father by his sacrifice, nor acquit us from the charge of guilt, nor, in short, perform the office of priest, unless he had been very God, because no human ability was equal to such a burden, it is however certain, that he performed all these things in his human nature ... righteousness was manifested to us in his flesh ... he places the fountain of righteousness entirely in the incarnation of Christ, 'He has made him to be sin for us who knew no sin, that we might be made the righteousness of God in him" (2 Cor. 5:21).'" *Institutes of the Christian Religion* 3.11.9.

107 C.S. Lewis, *Letters to Malcolm: Chiefly on Prayer* (New York: Harcourt, 1992), 108.

108 *On the Resurrection of the Flesh*, 43.

109 St. Augustine, *City of God* 21.16.

110 E.P. Sanders, *Judaism: Practice and Belief, 63 BCE–66 CE* (Minneapolis: Fortress Press, 2016), 448.

111 See "Inscription of Abercius," *The New Catholic Encyclopedia*.

112 Alfons Zettler and Eva-Maria Butz, "Pilgrim's Devotion? Christian Graffiti from Antiquity to the Middle Ages," in

Travel, Pilgrimage and Social Interaction from Antiquity to the Middle Ages, eds. Jenni Kuuliala and Jussi Rantala (New York: Routledge, 2021), 146.

113 *Panarion* 75.8.

114 See for example Zelda Caldwell, "Pope Francis Appoints Pro-Abortion Economist to Pontifical Academy for Life" Catholic News Agency (October 18, 2022), Available online at: https://www.catholicnewsagency.com/news/252577/pope-francis-appoints-pro-abortion-economist-to-pontifical-academy-for-life.

115 Francis X. Rocca, "Suspense, Planning During Interregnum" *The Tablet* (March 6, 2013). Available online at: https://thetablet.org/suspense-planning-during-interregnum/?gated=true.

116 See "Stances of Faiths on LGBTQ+ Issues: Old Catholics/Independent Catholics," available online at: https://www.hrc.org/resources/stances-of-faiths-on-lgbt-issues-old-catholics-independent-catholics.

117 *First Apology*, 46.

118 *City of God*, 13.7.

119 *De virtute fidei divinae*, disp. 20, n. 149, pp. 566-567.

120 Angelo Amato, Responses to Some Questions Regarding Certain Aspects of the Doctrine on the Church, June 29, 2007.

121 *Luther's Works*, 30:190.